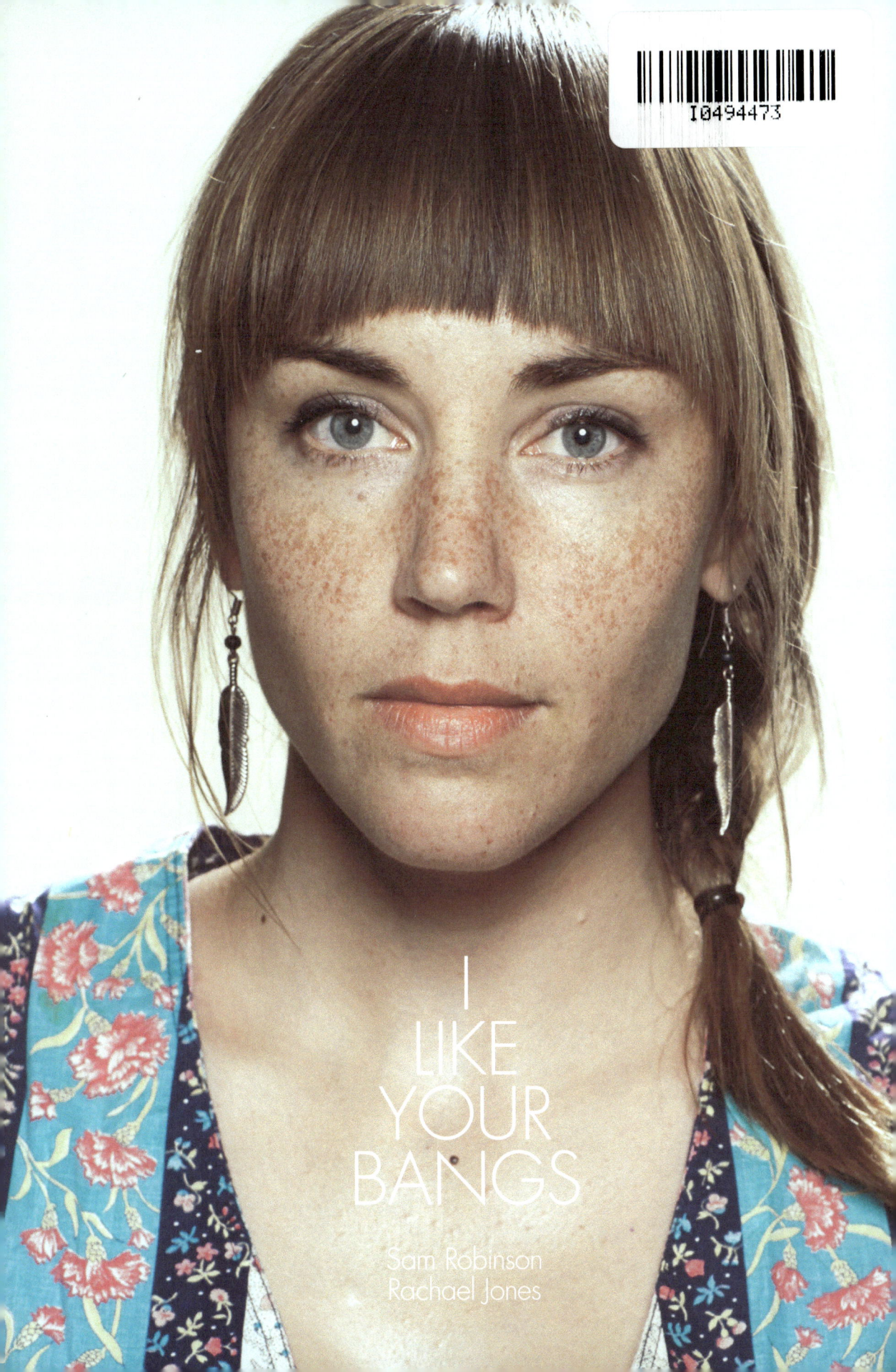

I
LIKE
YOUR
BANGS

Sam Robinson
Rachael Jones

"I Like Your Bangs," by Sam Robinson and Rachael Jones. ISBN 978-0-692-40025-8 (softcover).

Published 2015 by Sam Robinson Photography and Virtualbookworm.com Publishing Inc., P.O. Box 9949, College Station, TX 77842, US. ©2015, Sam Robinson. All rights reserved. No part of this publication may be reproduced, stored in a retrieval system, or transmitted in any form or by any means, electronic, mechanical, recording or otherwise, without the prior written permission of Sam Robinson and Rachael Jones.

I
LIKE
YOUR
BANGS

Sam Robinson
Rachael Jones

'Whether you wanted to look younger, sexier, or more creative, the decision to get bangs can be terrifying and invigorating in equal measure.'

Intro

For some, it's the spontaneous result of a bad breakup. "I'm ready for a change!" you shout to your stylist, convinced that this new look will change your life forever. For others, it's a carefully planned, Pinterest-researched decision that only happens when everything feels just right. Countless times you have stared in the mirror, sweeping the ends of your hair up to your forehead to visualize the style.

Whether you wanted to look younger, sexier, or more creative, the decision to get bangs can be terrifying and invigorating in equal measure.

Bang lovers remain fearless and seem to march to the beat of their own drum ignoring the fashion magazines that tell them, "Straight bangs are out" or to stay bang-less because of the shape of their face. They laugh at the thought that they might regret the cut and remain unfazed by the potential awkwardness that can come when growing them out.

I'm with them. I still consider it one of my greatest personal triumphs to have grown out my straight-cut bangs without caving in and getting a trim. But I don't care who you are, by the time you finally grow out your bangs, you never fail to feel that urge to cut them again. There's just something about this flirty hairstyle that keeps you coming back for more.

The look is nothing new, but that's probably why it holds such retro charm. Through the centuries, bangs have been a 'go-to' hairstyle. In the 1920s, Louise Brooks was one of the first iconic women to sport the blunt bang (paired with a short bob, of course).

In every decade since there have been superstar supporters of every bang trend going. And thanks to the indie doe-eyed darling, Zooey Deschanel, who continues to rock the bangs with effortless quirk - bangs are here to stay.

So where better to witness a broad spectrum of the fearless living out their bang phase than the place where women and men flock to rock their personal style – Austin, Texas during the SXSW music festival. The city pulls in a mixed bag of bang addicts – those who have been flaunting their bangs almost since they were born and those who have just discovered them.

If you're looking for a little 'bangspiration' of your own then look no further than these portraits taken of SXSW bang goers. You might just find yourself reaching for the phone to call your stylist. Or, if you're really brave, reaching for the scissors…

- Joanna Wilkinson

Lindsey Lee

I spent enough time in front of the mirror
holding my hair up and pretending to
have bangs. It was finally time to take
the plunge.

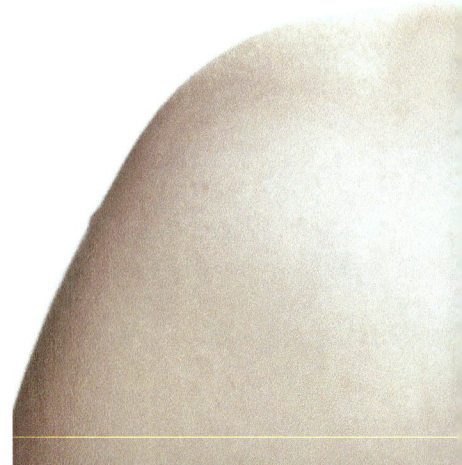

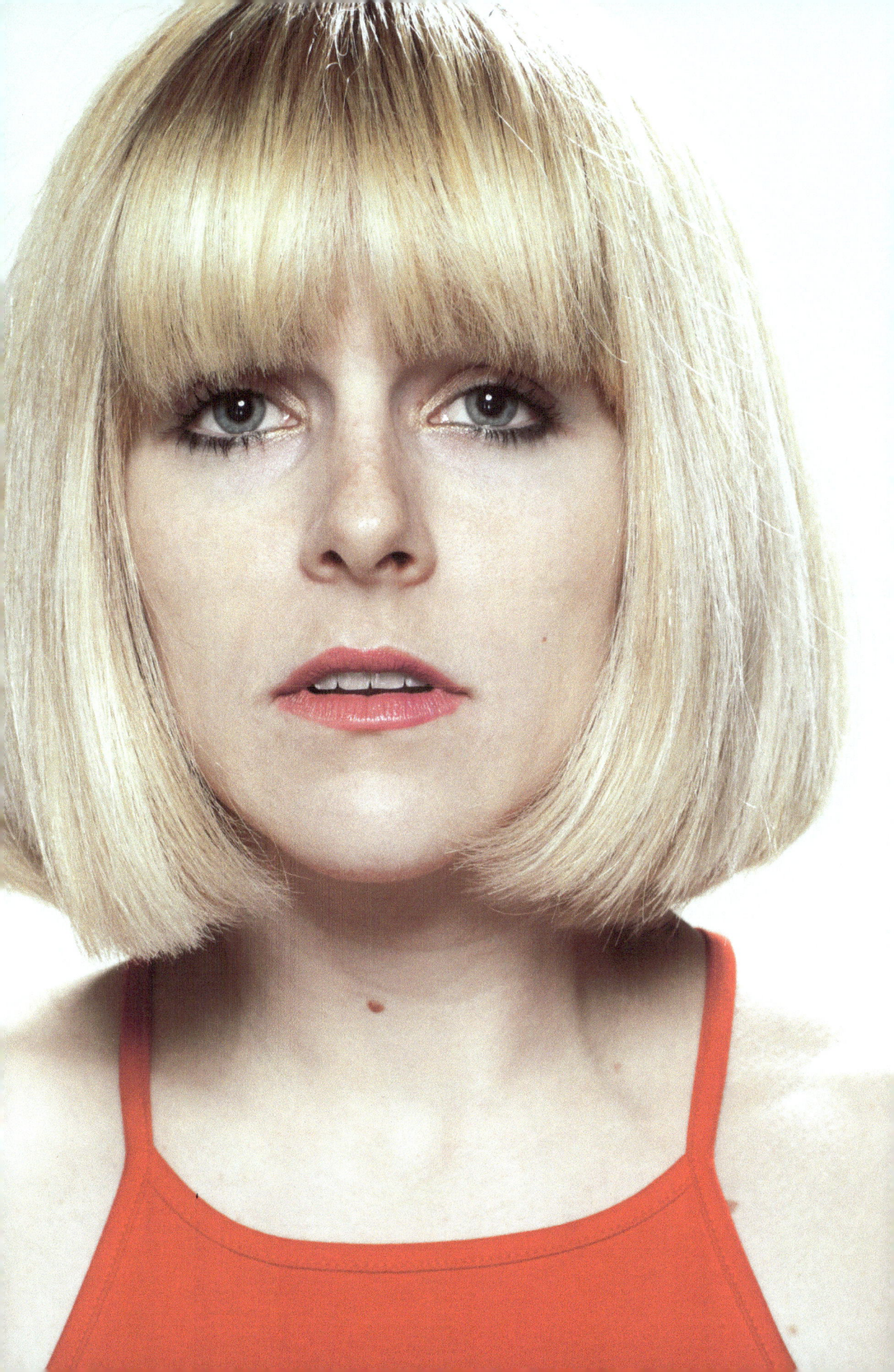

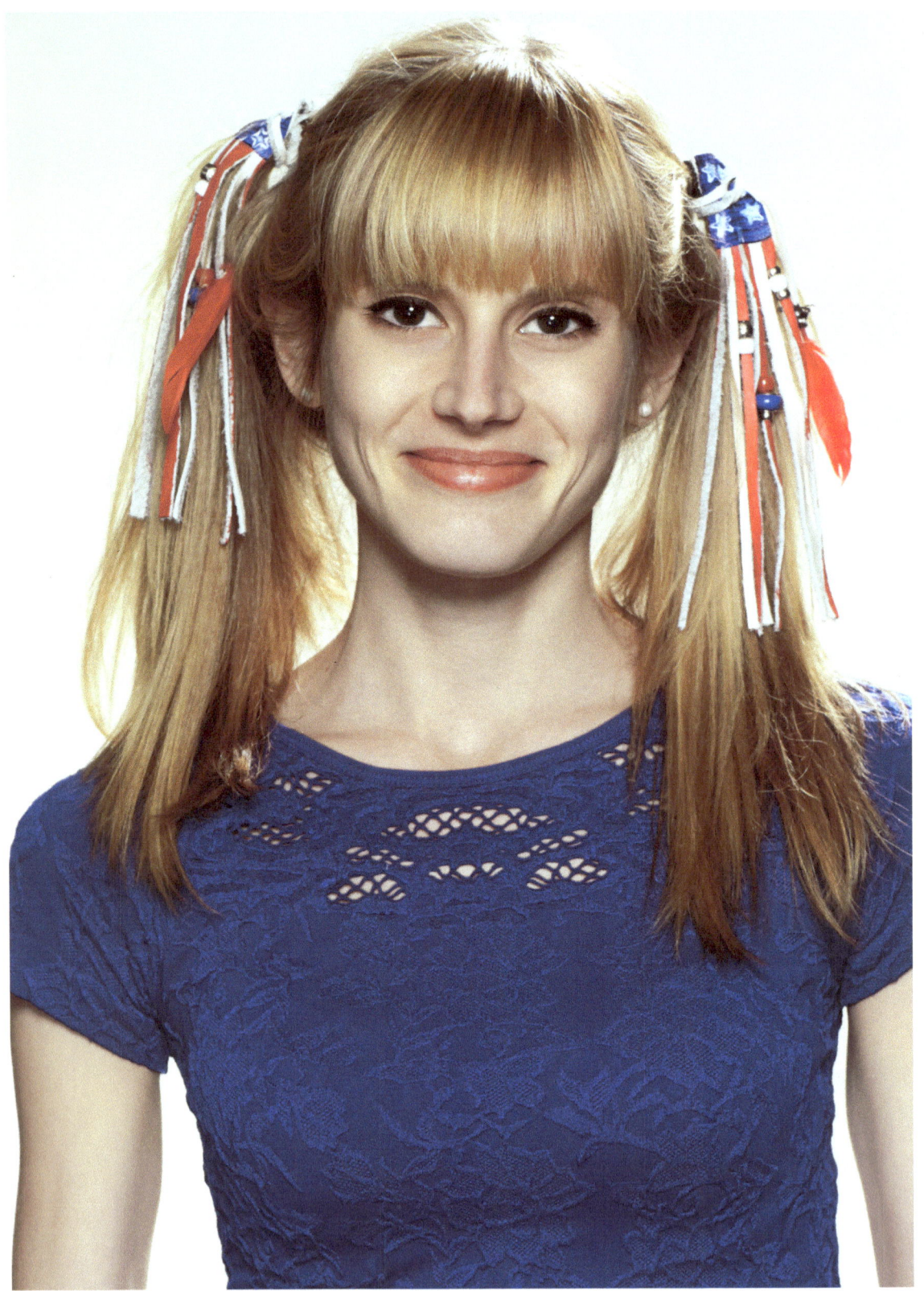

Casey Williams

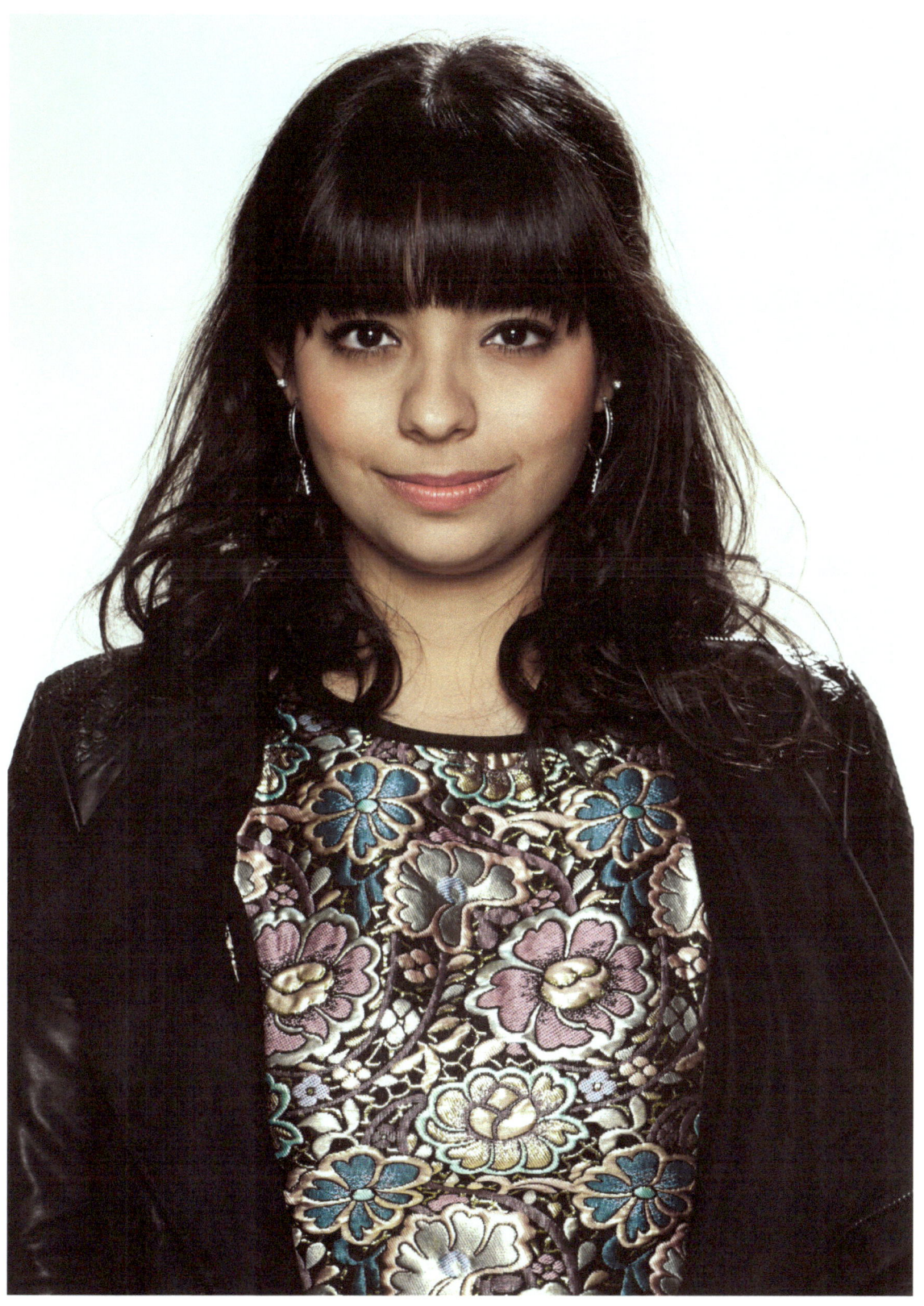

Jackie Cueller

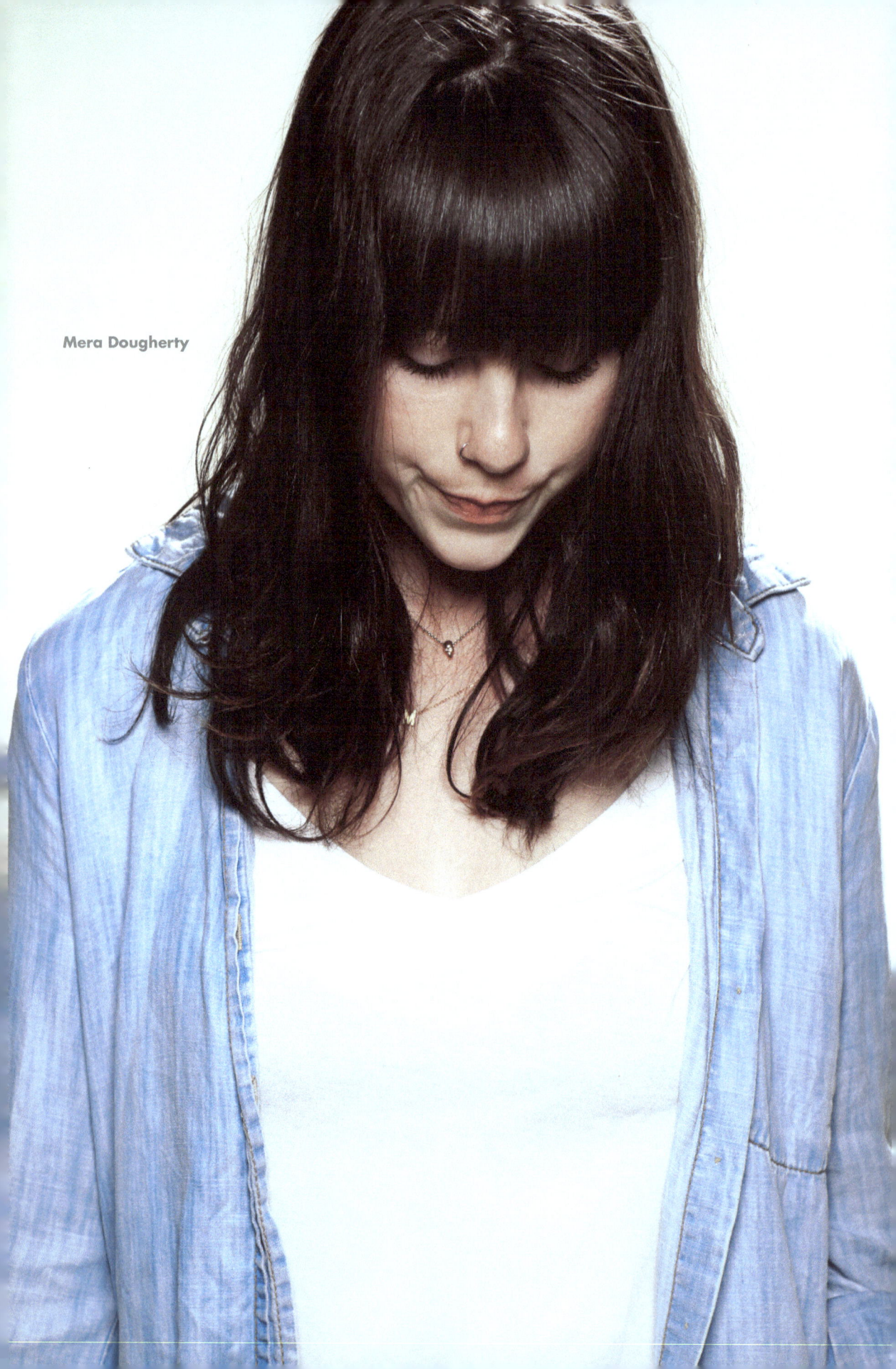

Mera Dougherty

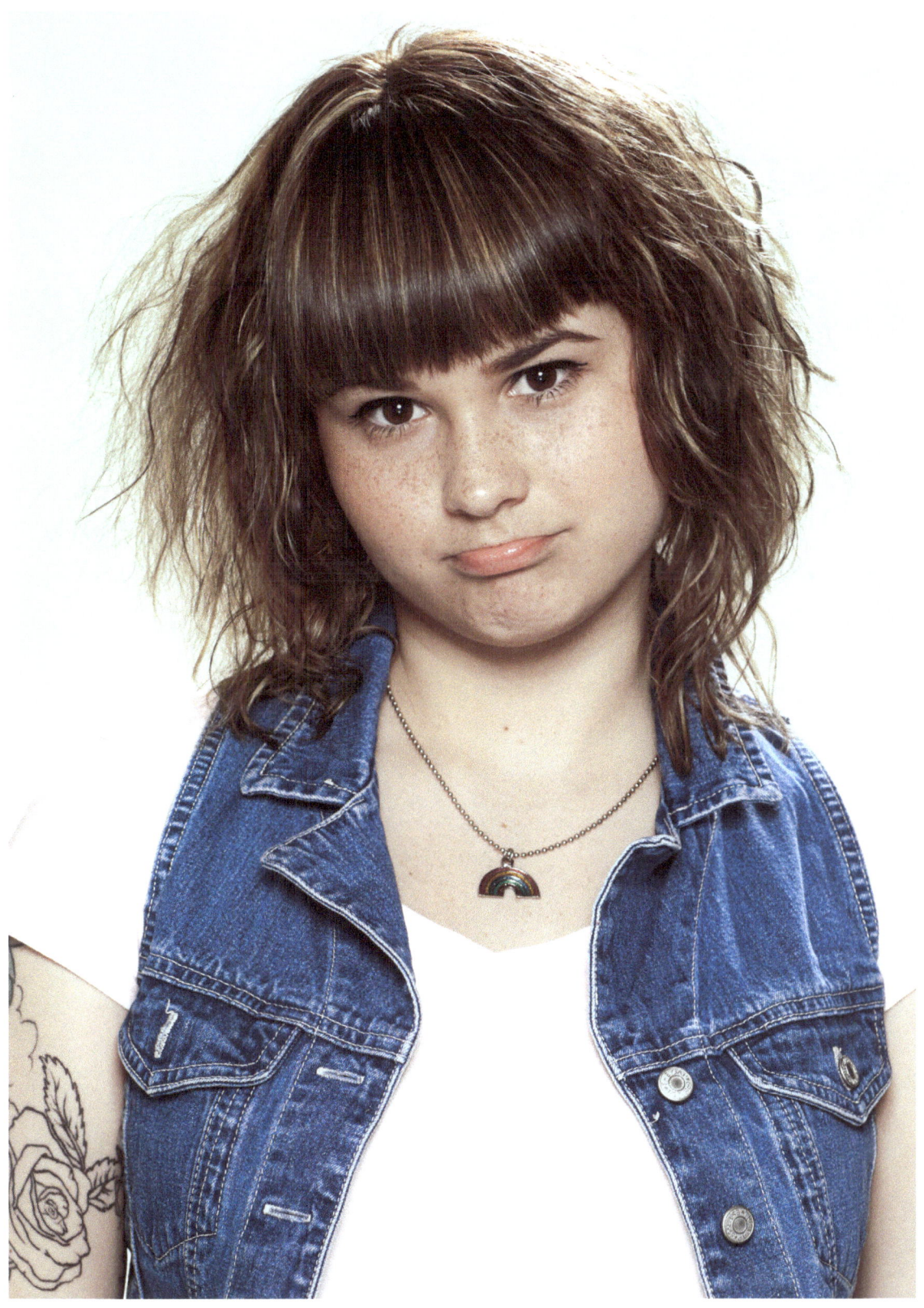

Trina Gear

Olivia Hjermitslev

I grew up in Denmark with a single dad who would cut corners to make ends meet. He would place me on the kitchen counter armed with these huge paper scissors. He would aim and make one long cut! The mothers at school would pity me, but I kind of liked the crazy straight yet completely uneven bangs and the ritual was fun.

I always tell the stylists not to give me cute bangs. I want straight, clean and cool but not punk rock hipster bangs! I guess it makes me feel a bit more like a woman more Danish in a foreign country, reminding me of my dad.

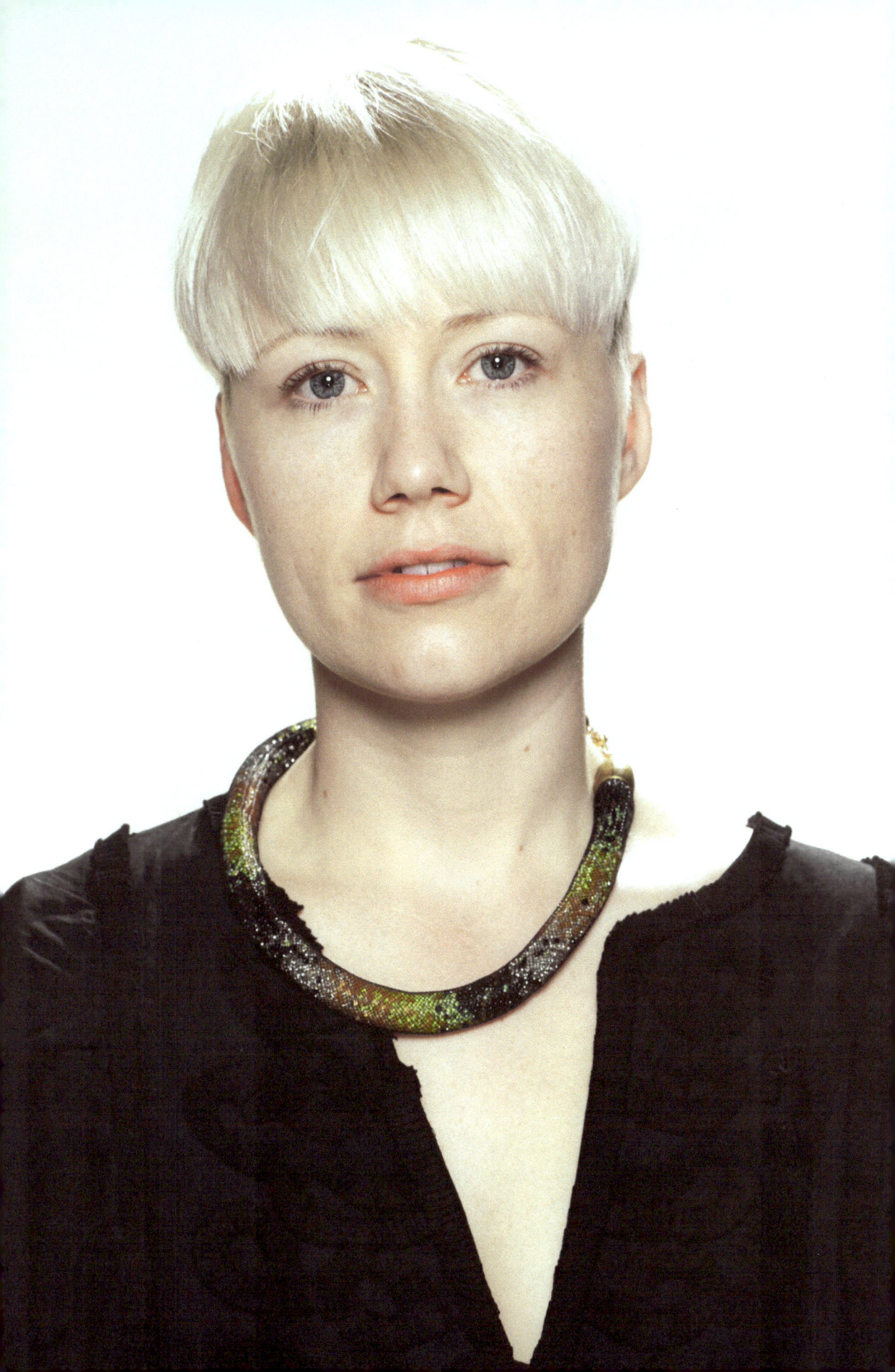

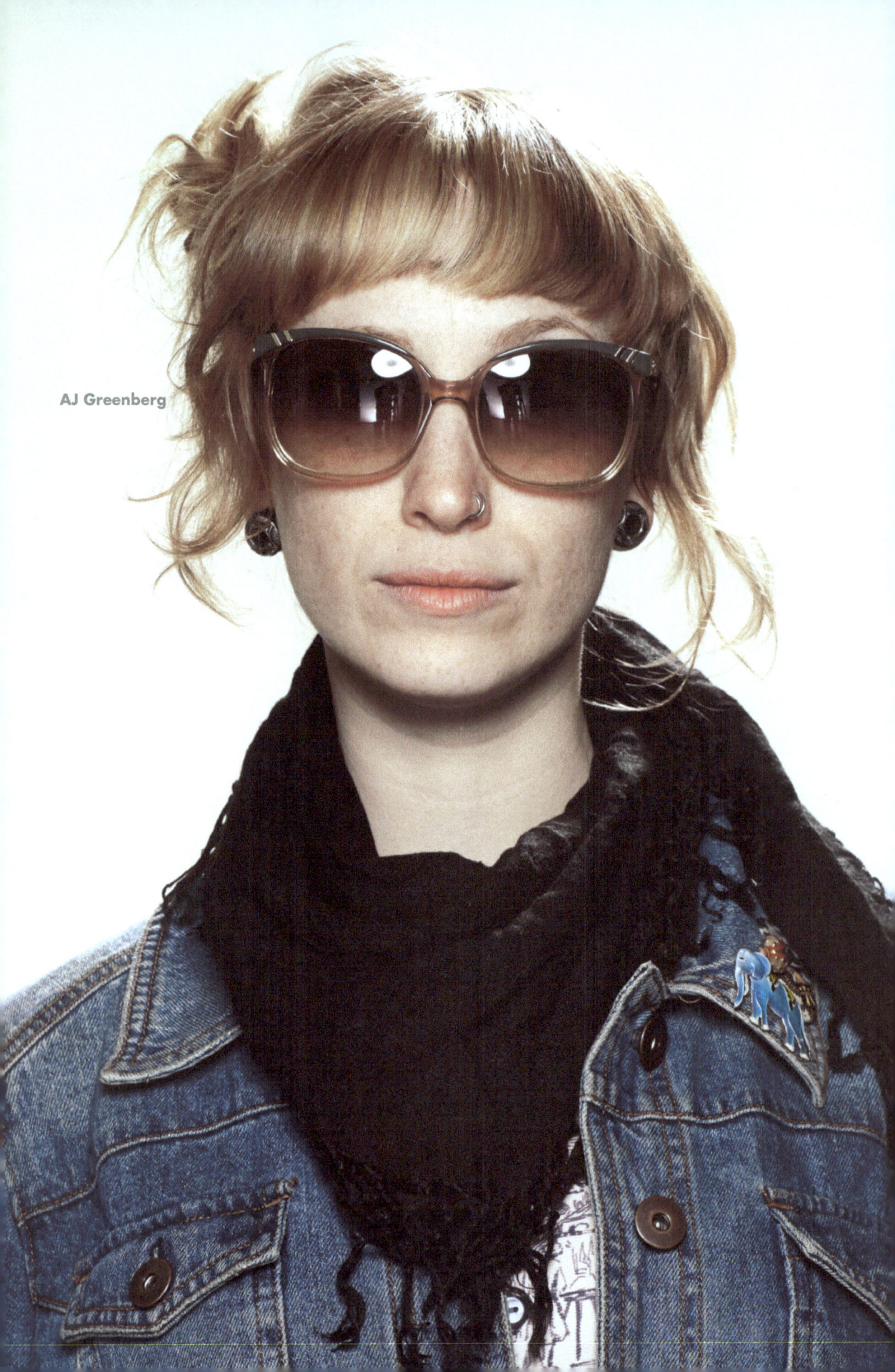

AJ Greenberg

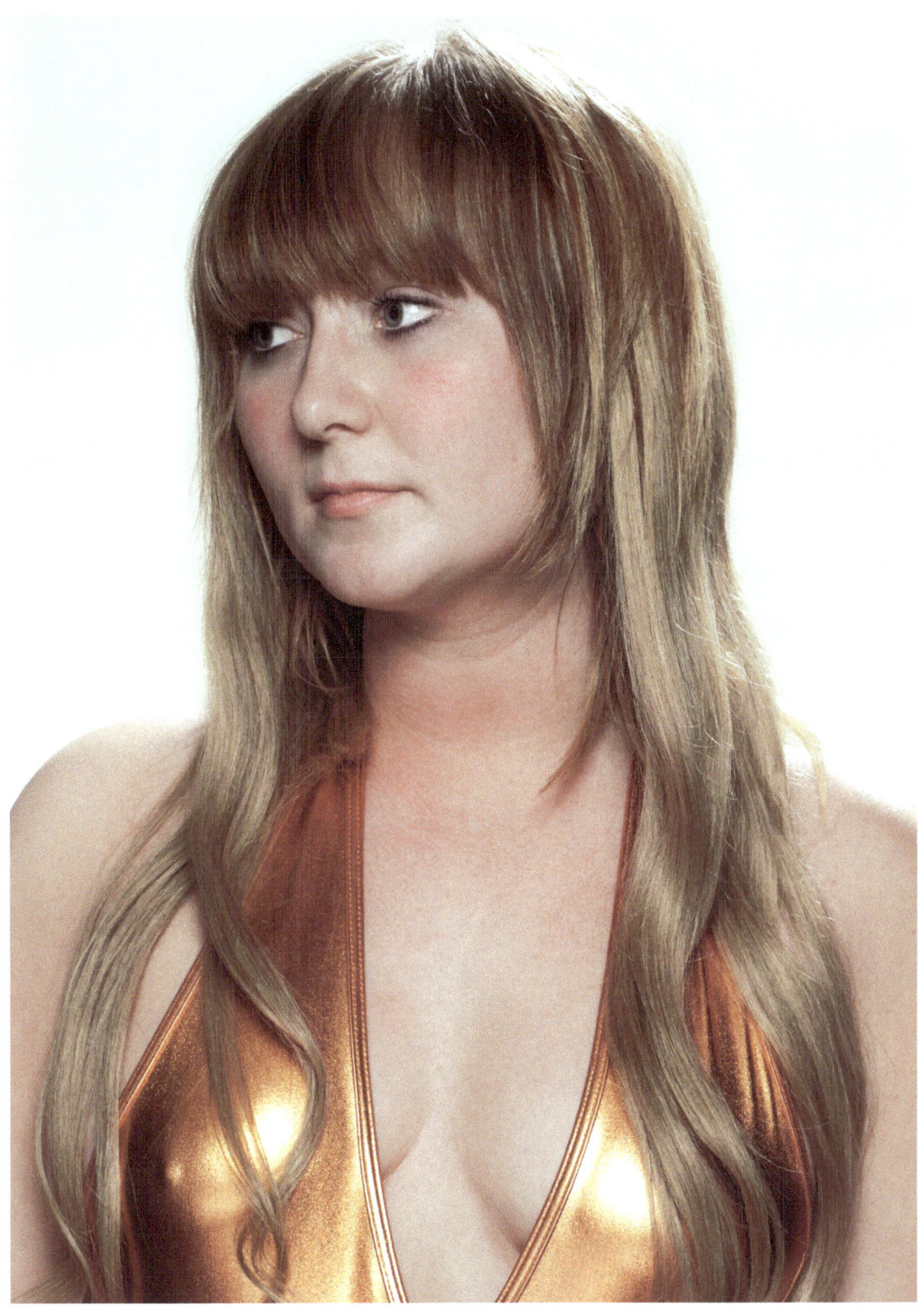

Stephanie Bird

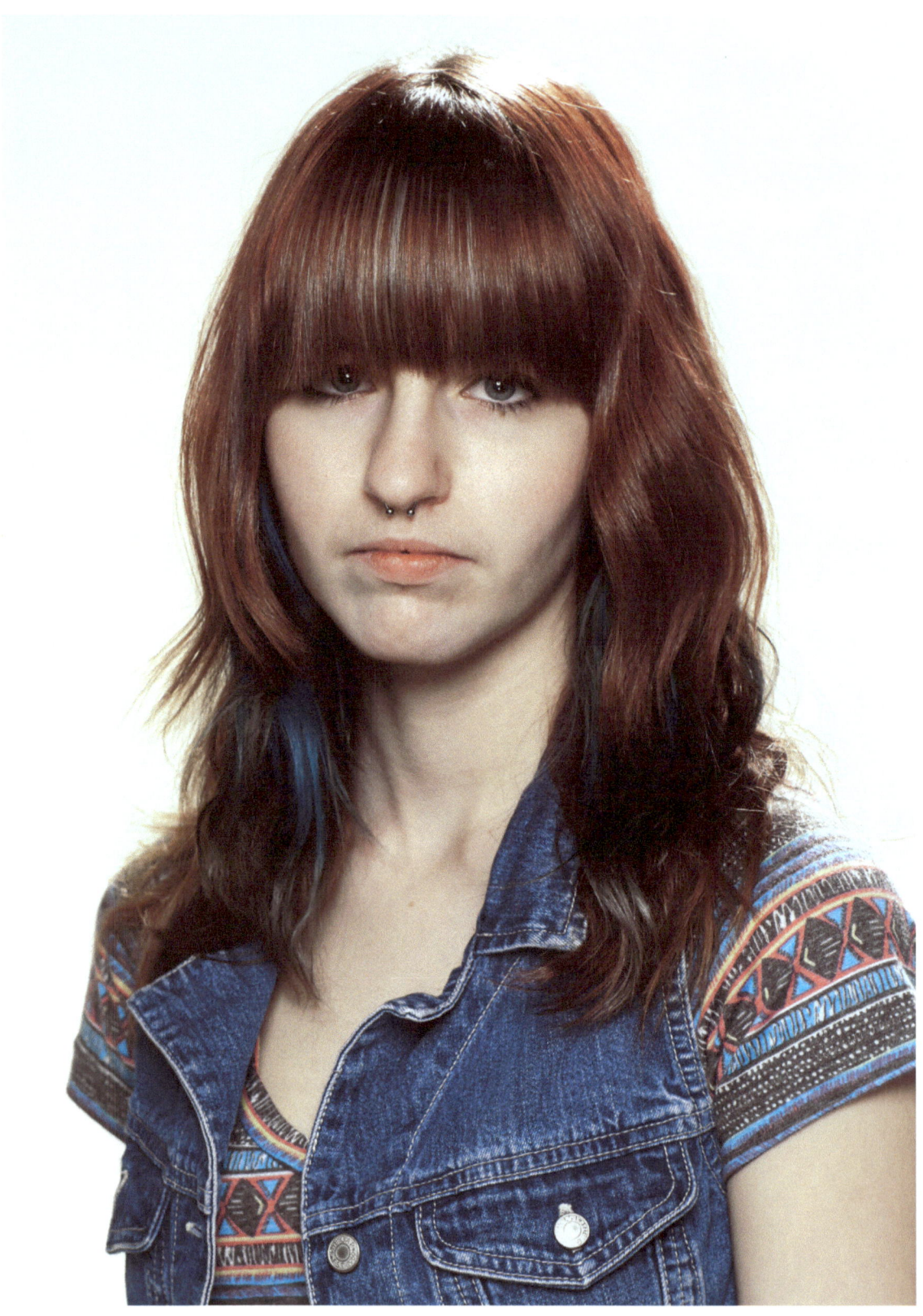

Emily Glisson

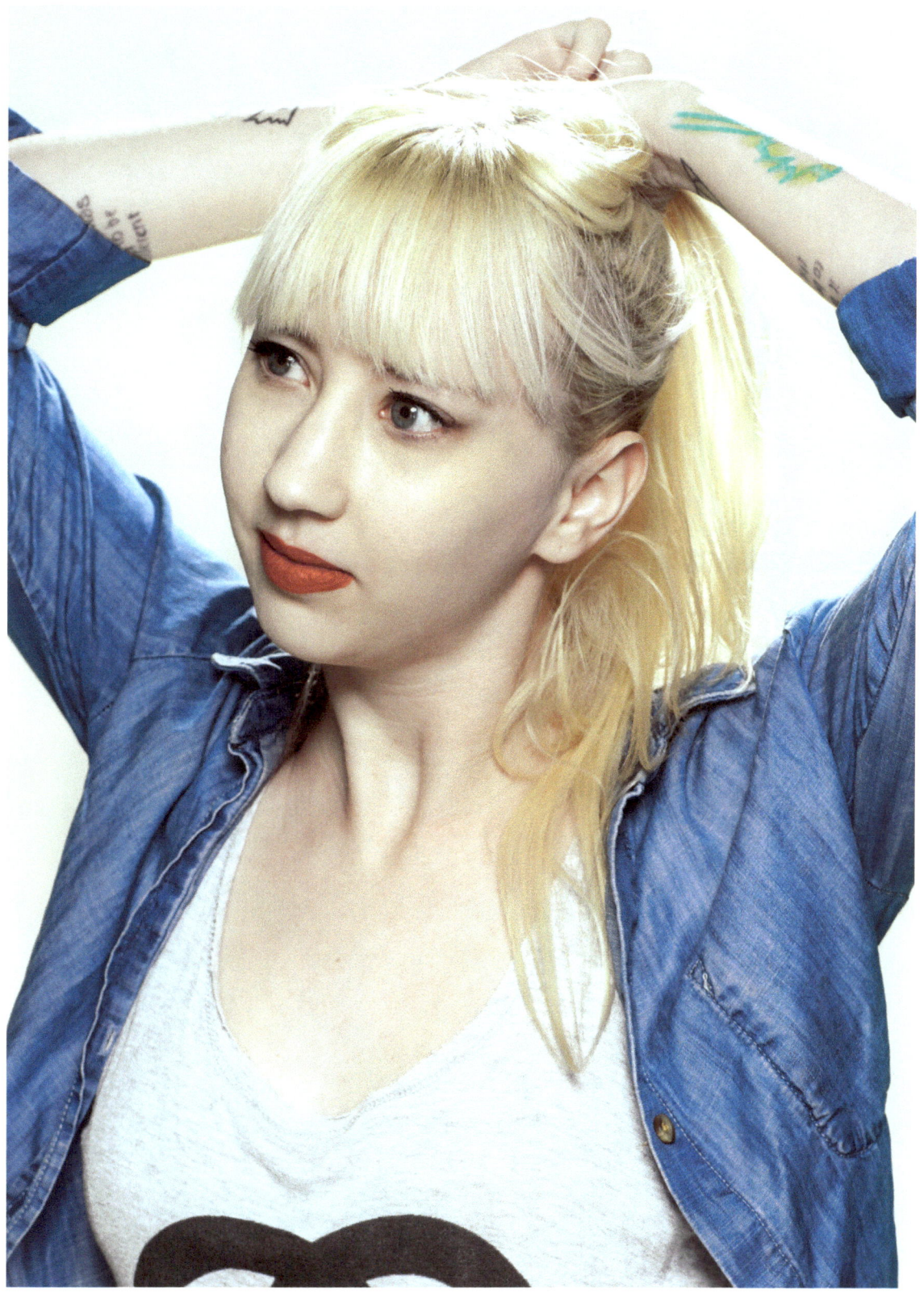

Elizabeth Speights

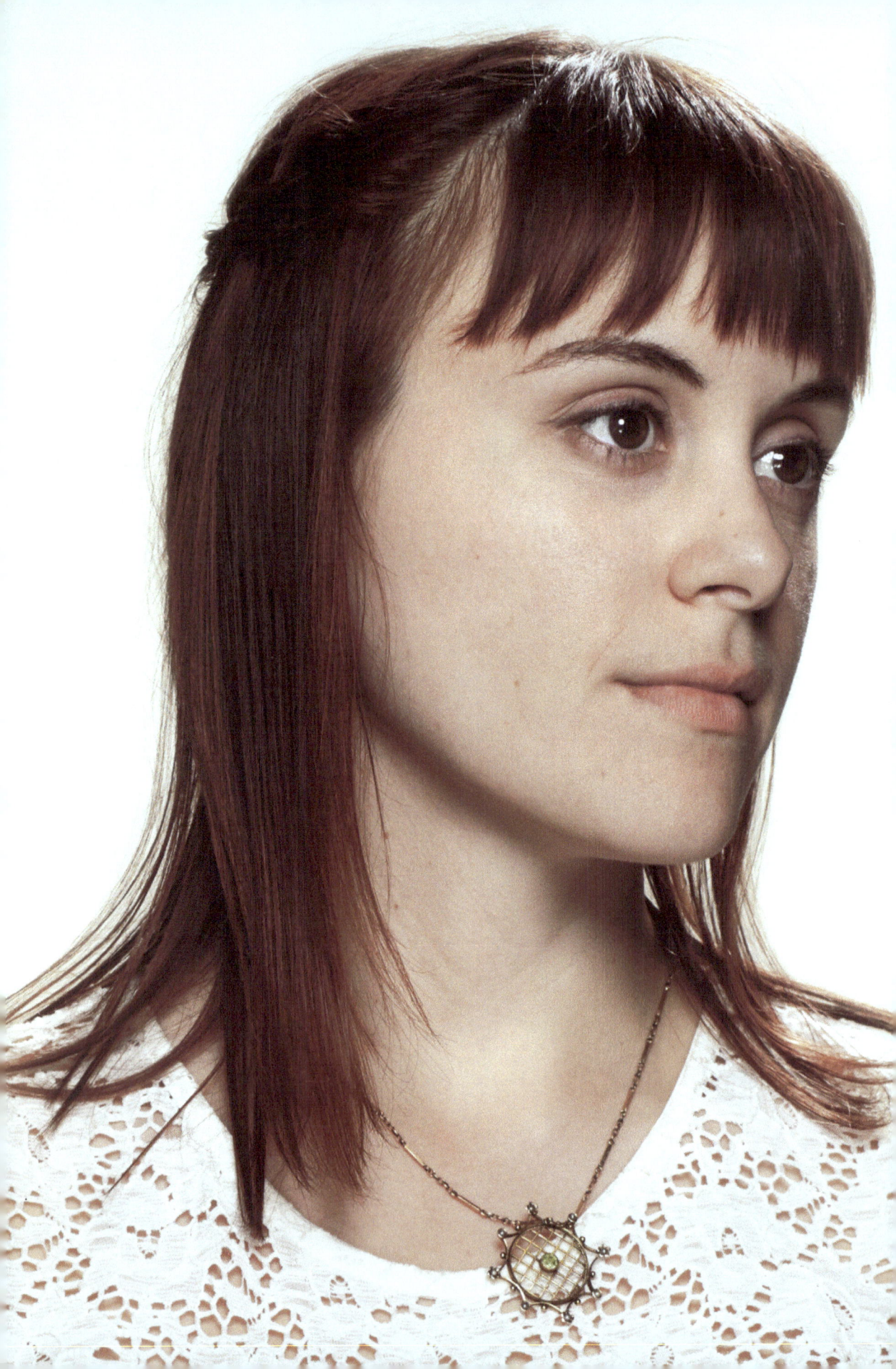

Baxter Buchanan

It can be a bewildering journey to find
the right set. You may convince yourself
bangs are frivolous and you're better off
changing your part, until you meet the
right stylist. Brushing the hair over your
eyes, they comb it to the side and ask,
"Are you sure about this?".

You hold their hand as they make the cut
with the other and it's then that your hair
finds its true calling.

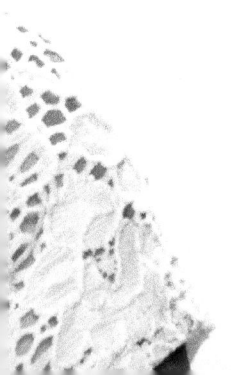

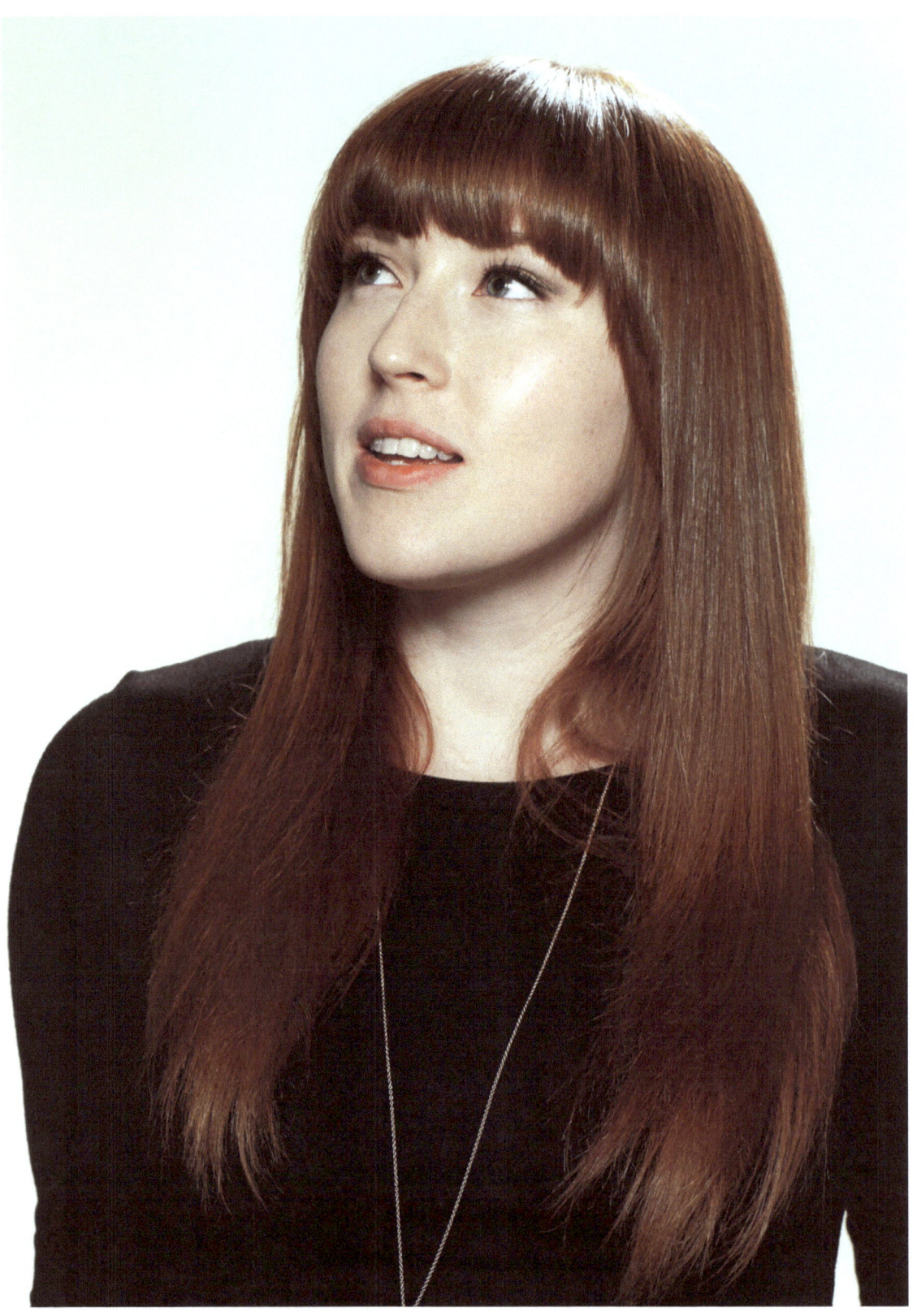

Tiffany Hollon

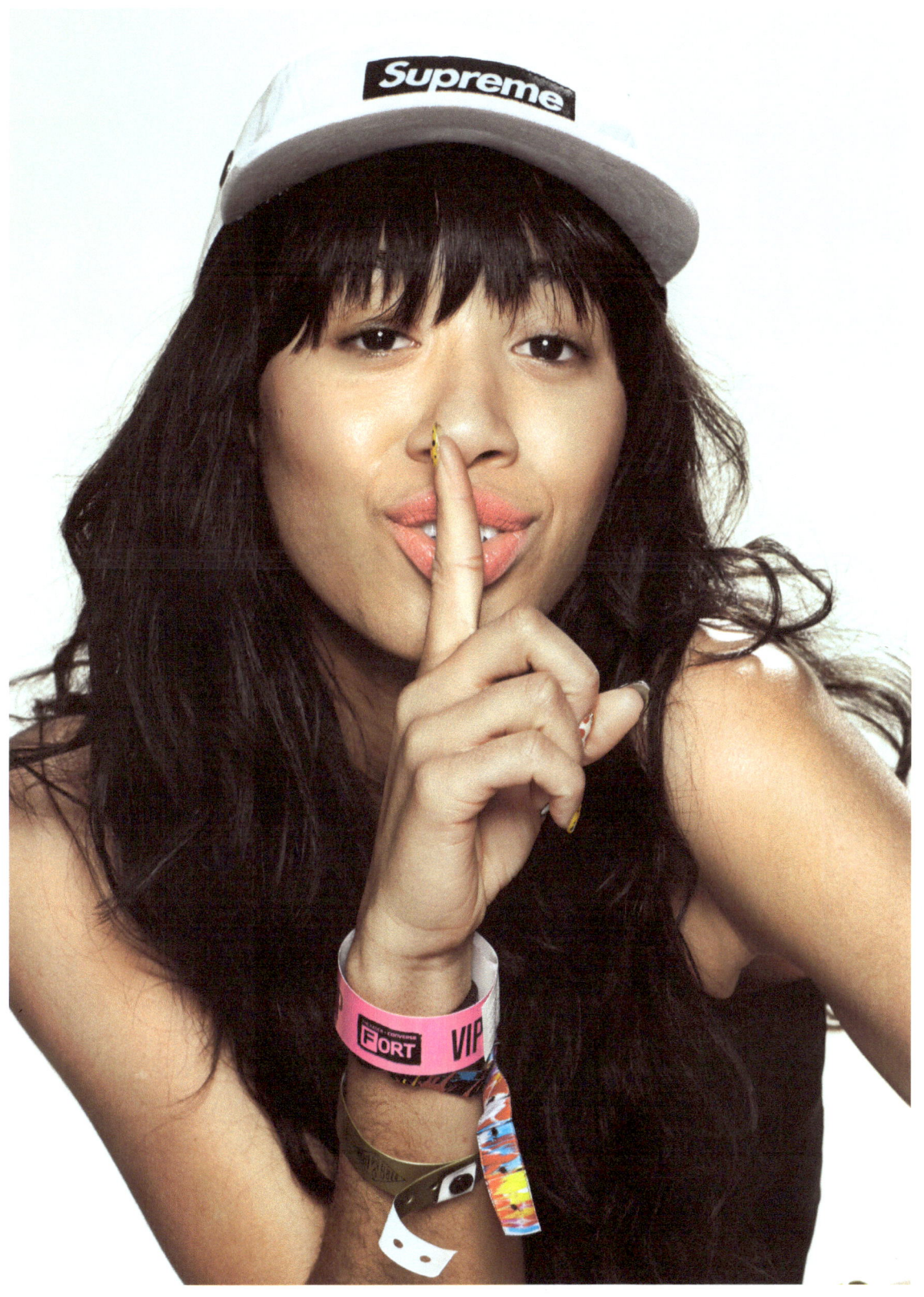

Kitty Cash

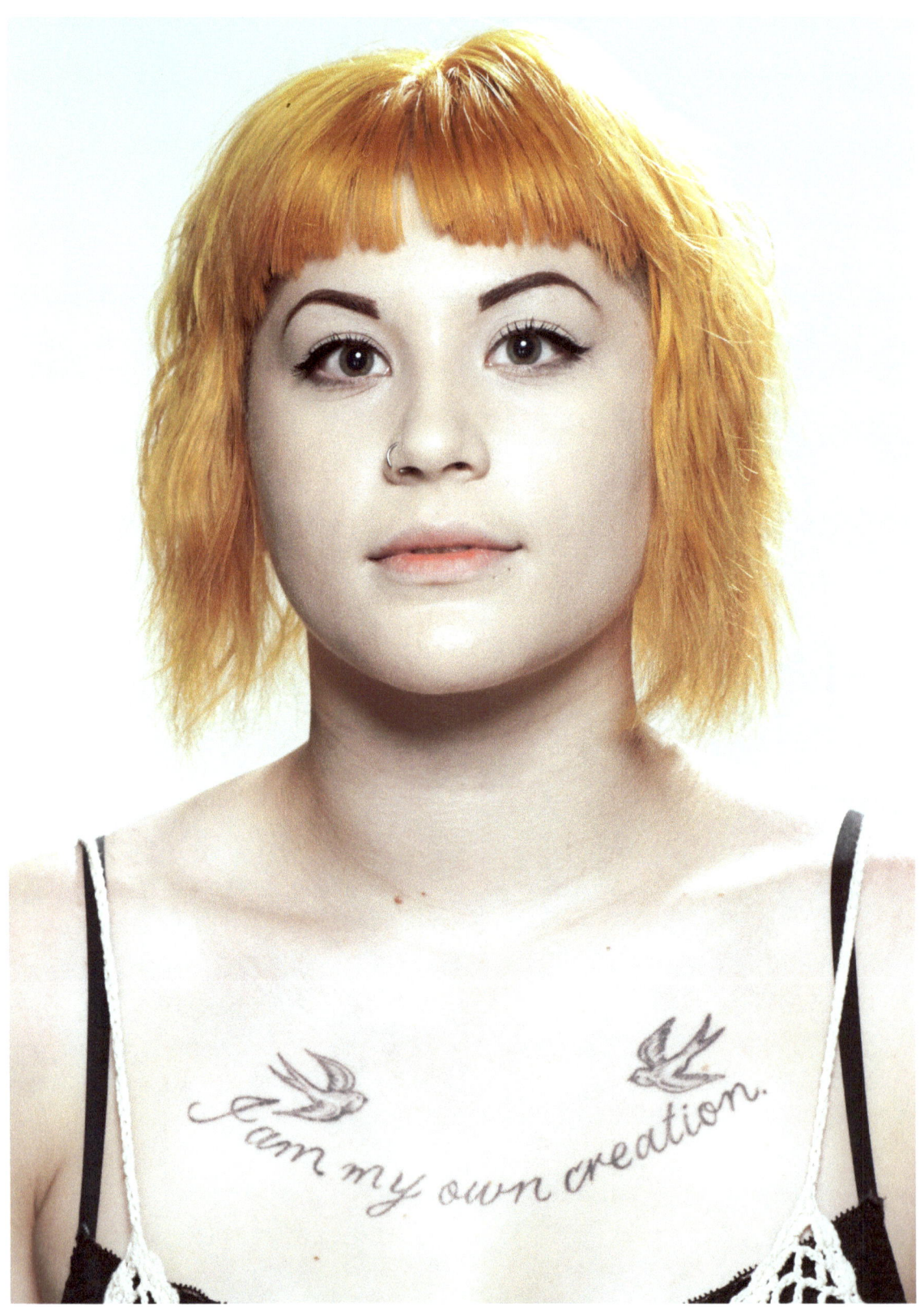

Samantha Evans

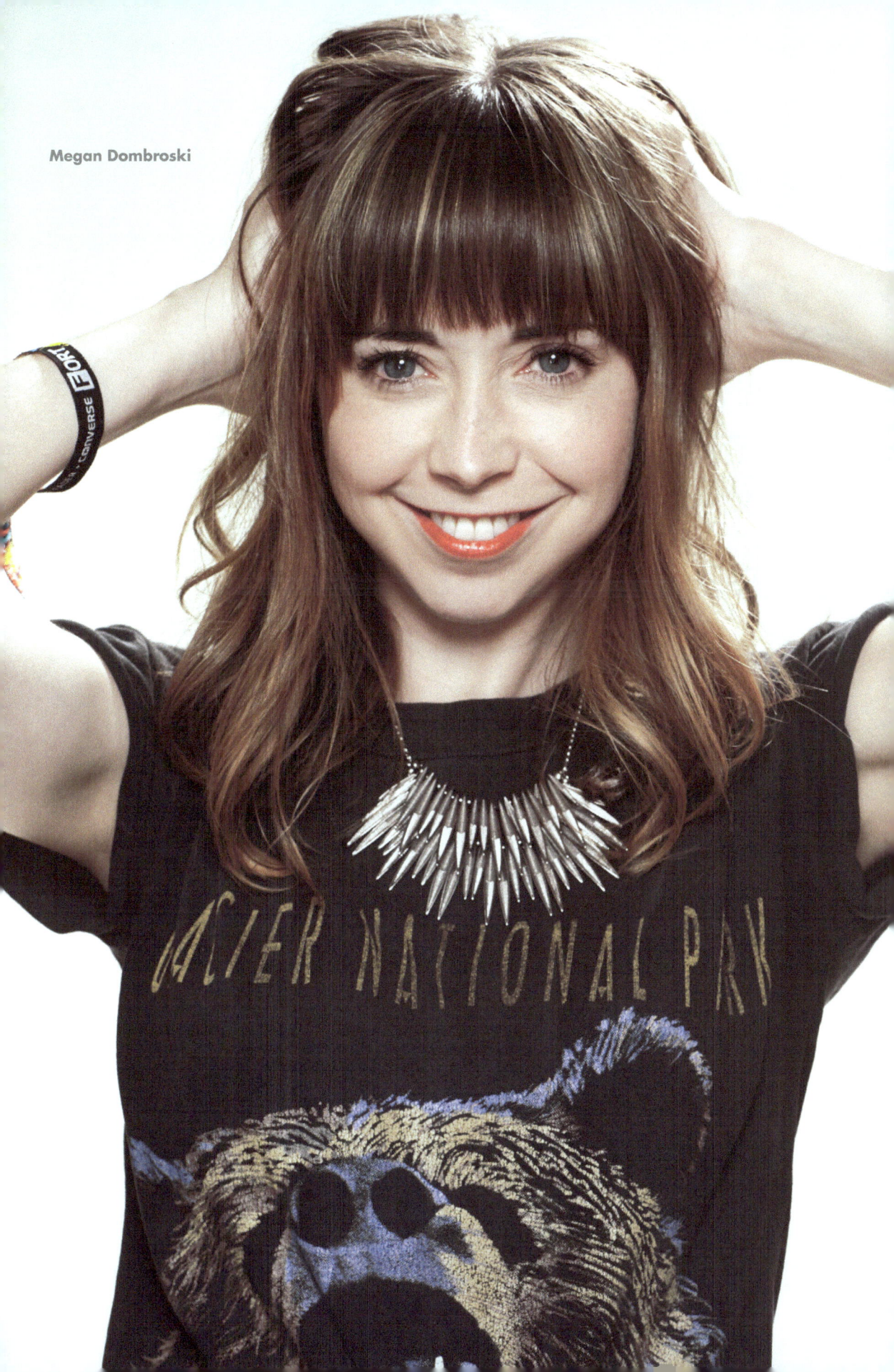

Megan Dombroski

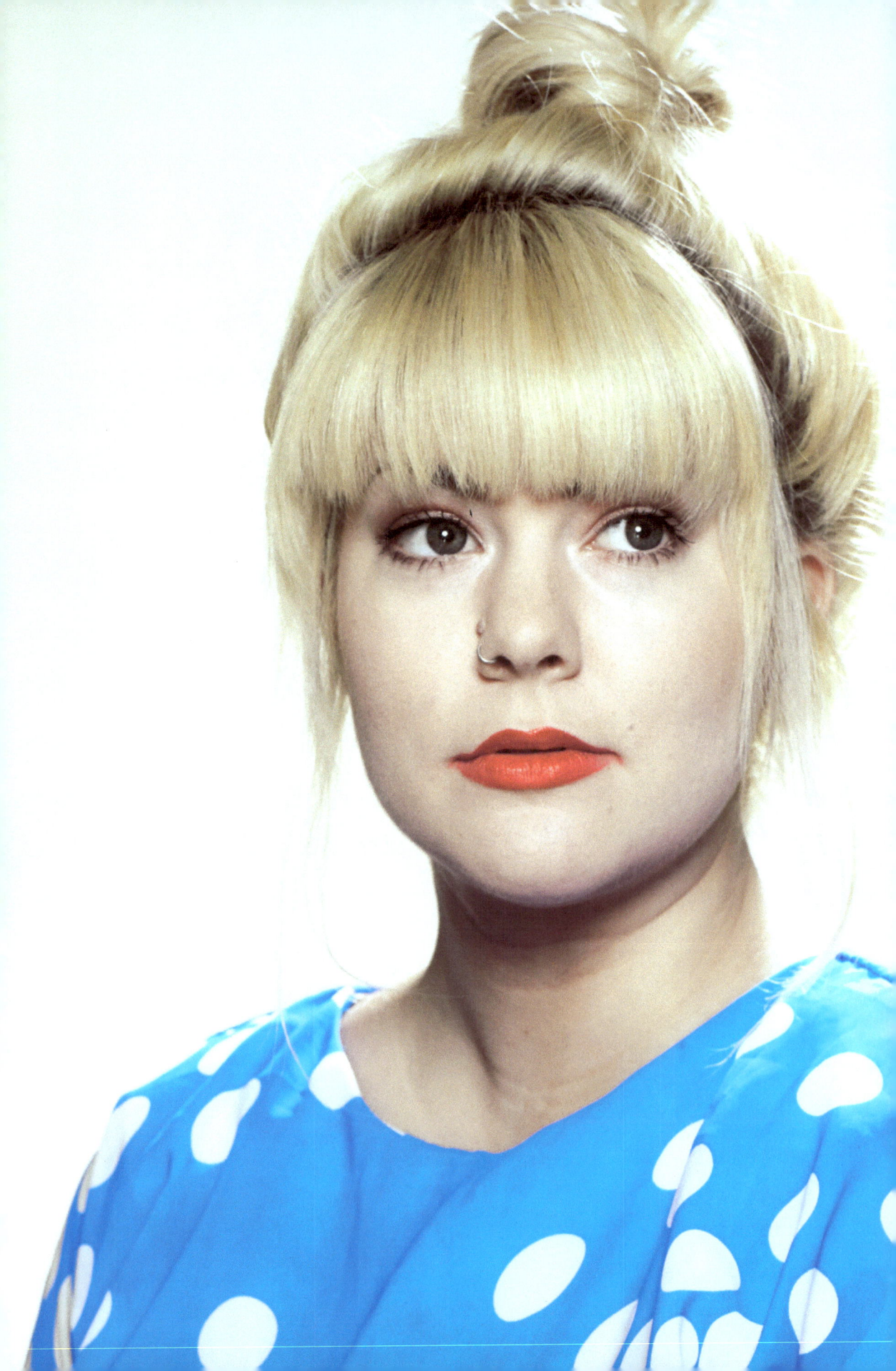

Audrey Brown

I just chopped them myself one day.
I had something in my head and they
helped me create a character.

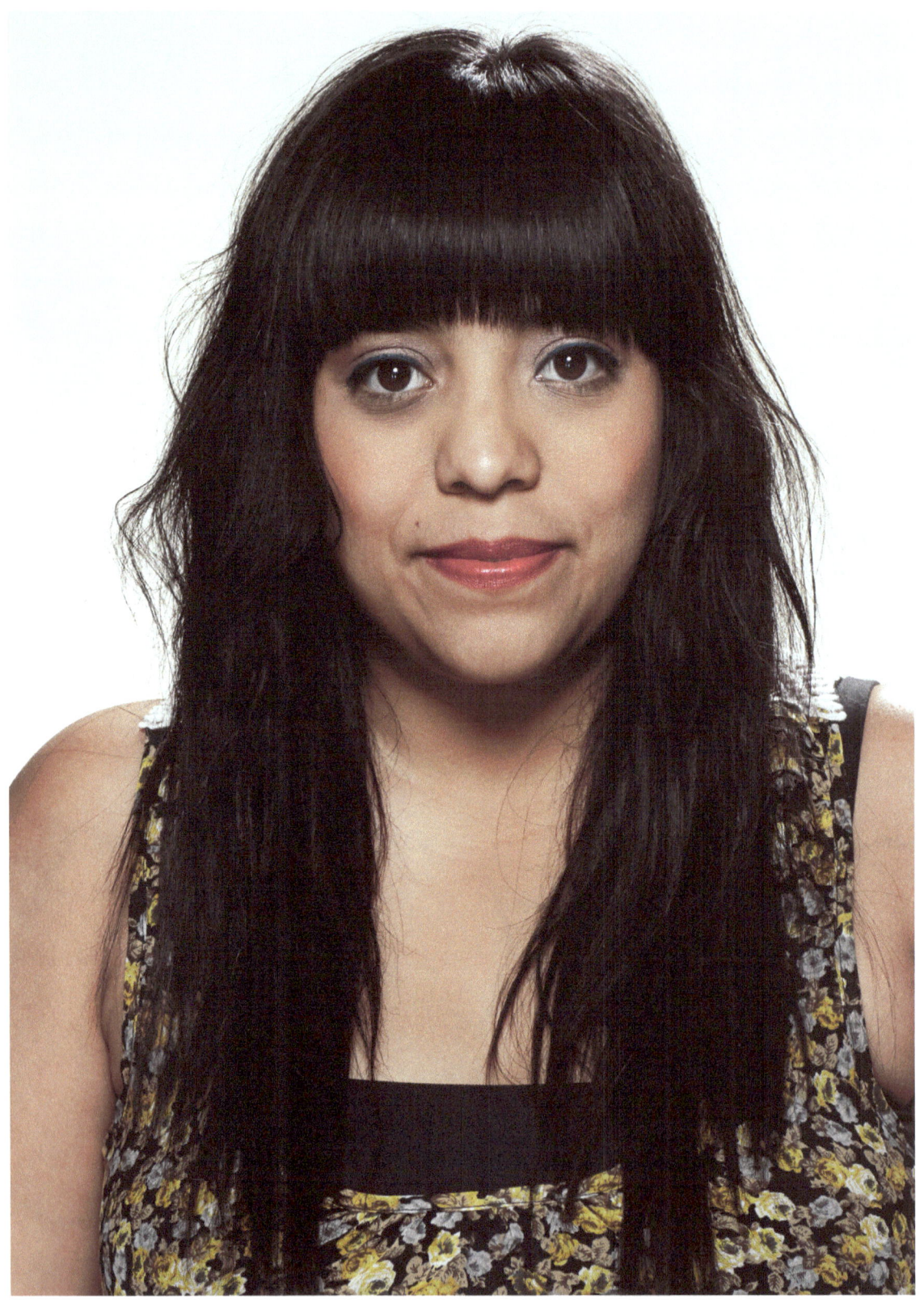

Chelsea Gonzales

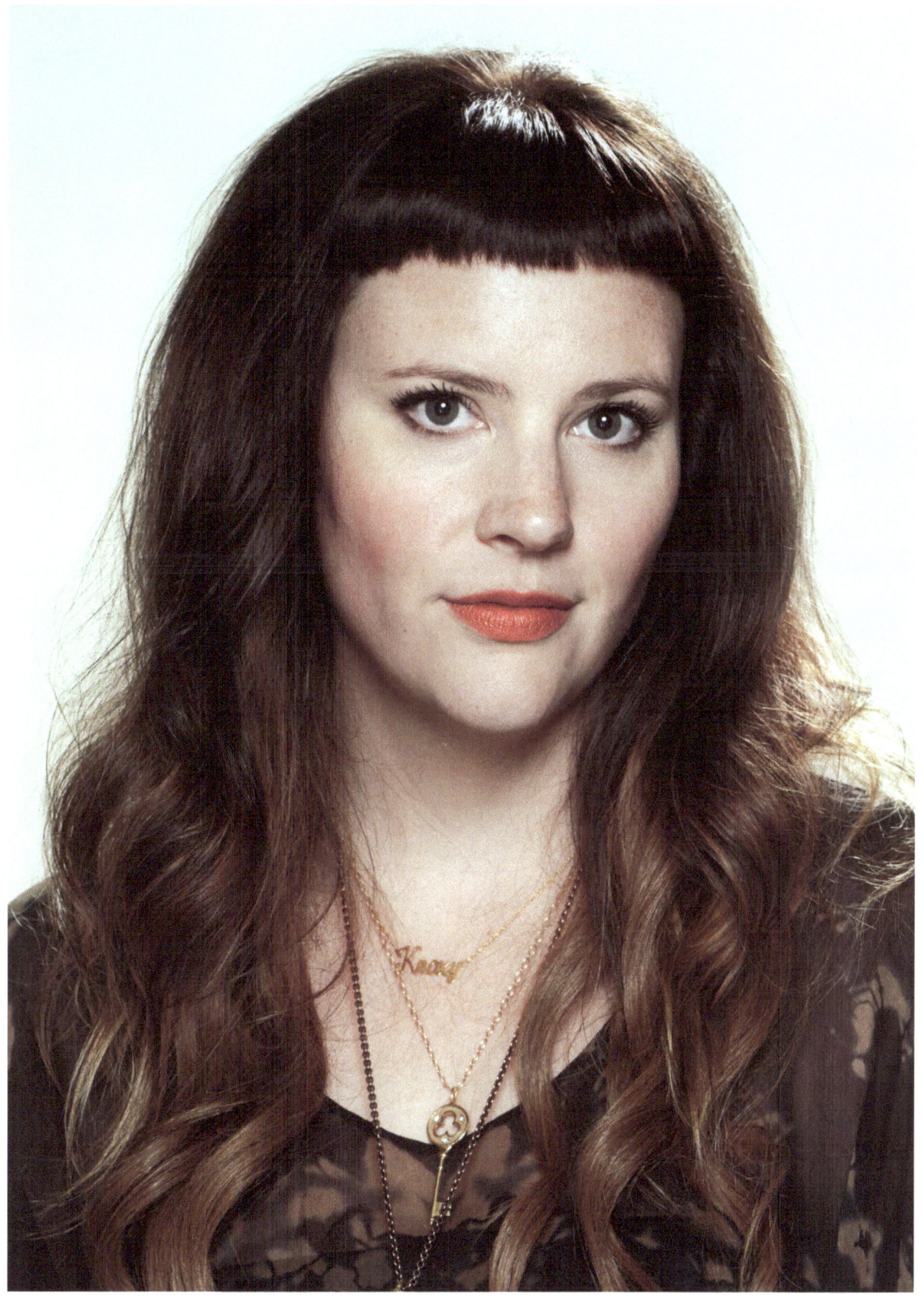

Knoxy Knox

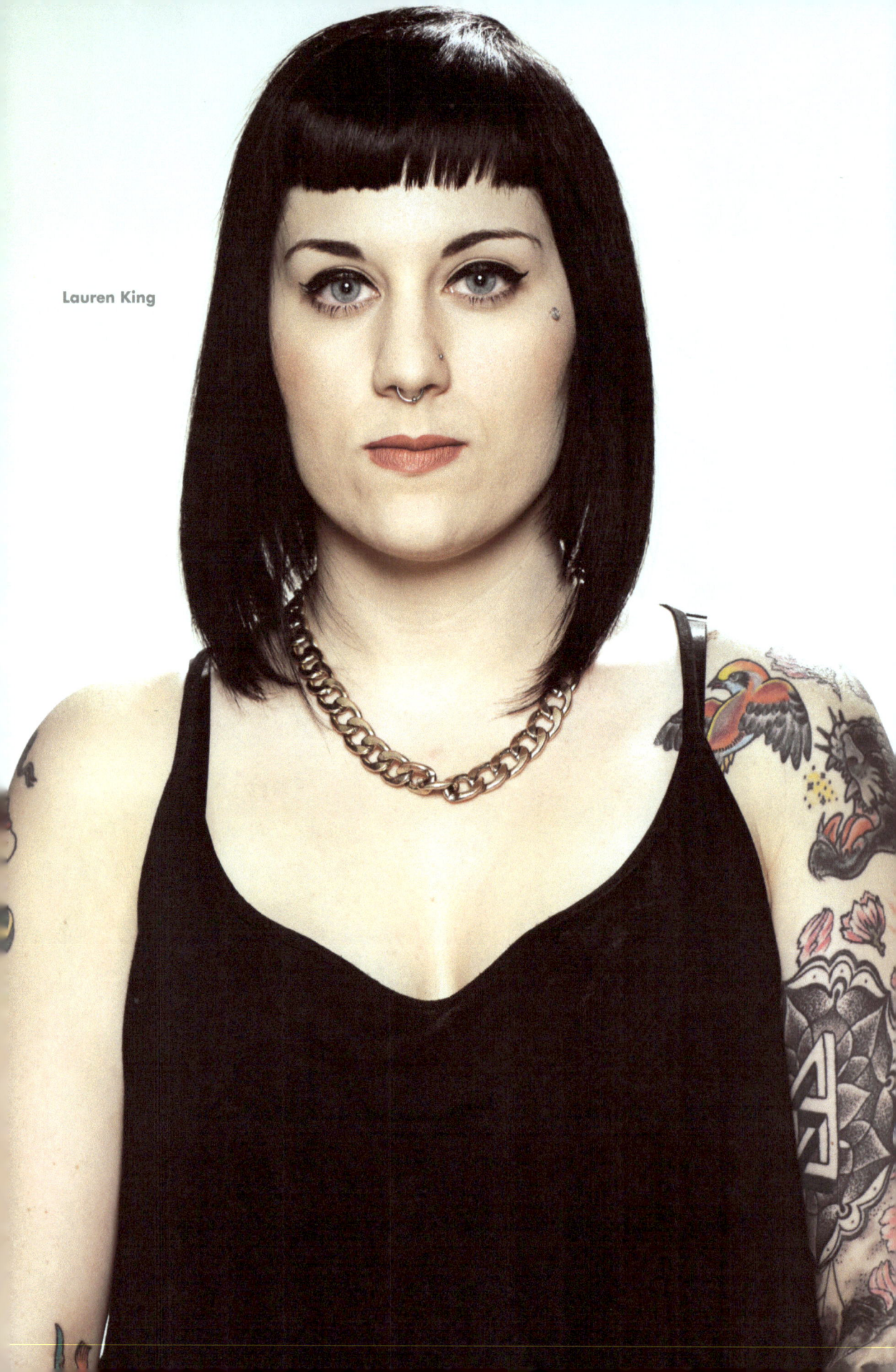

Lauren King

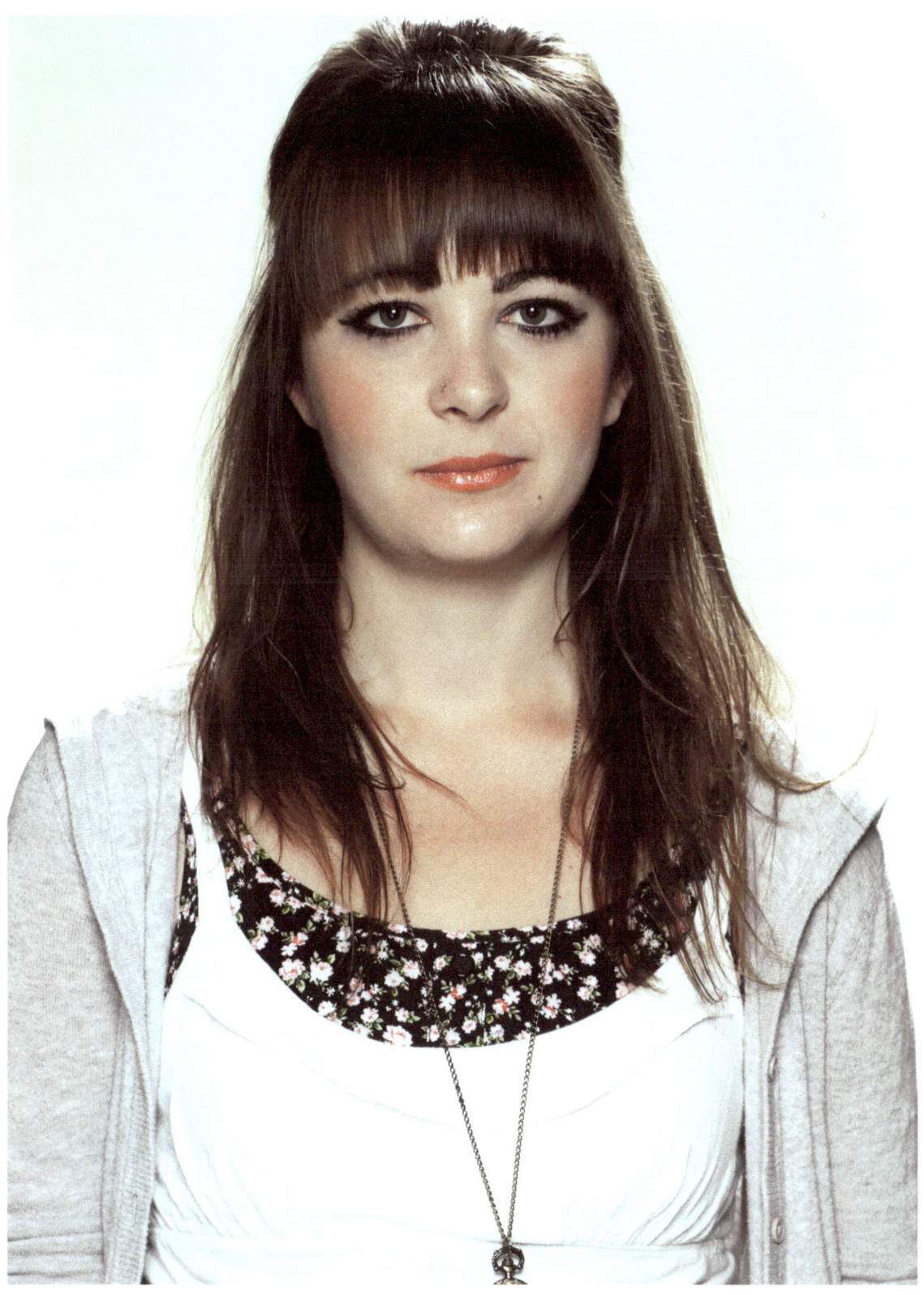

Erin Polsfoot

Mandy May

My bangs weren't always something
I preferred. Funny story is my 4 year
old daughter, Dresdin, got a hold of my
shears and cut her own hair.

I was upset at first, but then she told me
she only did it because she sees Mommy
cutting hair all the time.

To fix her experimental haircut, I had
to cut her bangs very short. She was not
very happy! So, in order for her to be
happy and feel pretty, I cut my bangs just
as short as hers!

Now, we both feel pretty with bangs
and we continue to wear them!

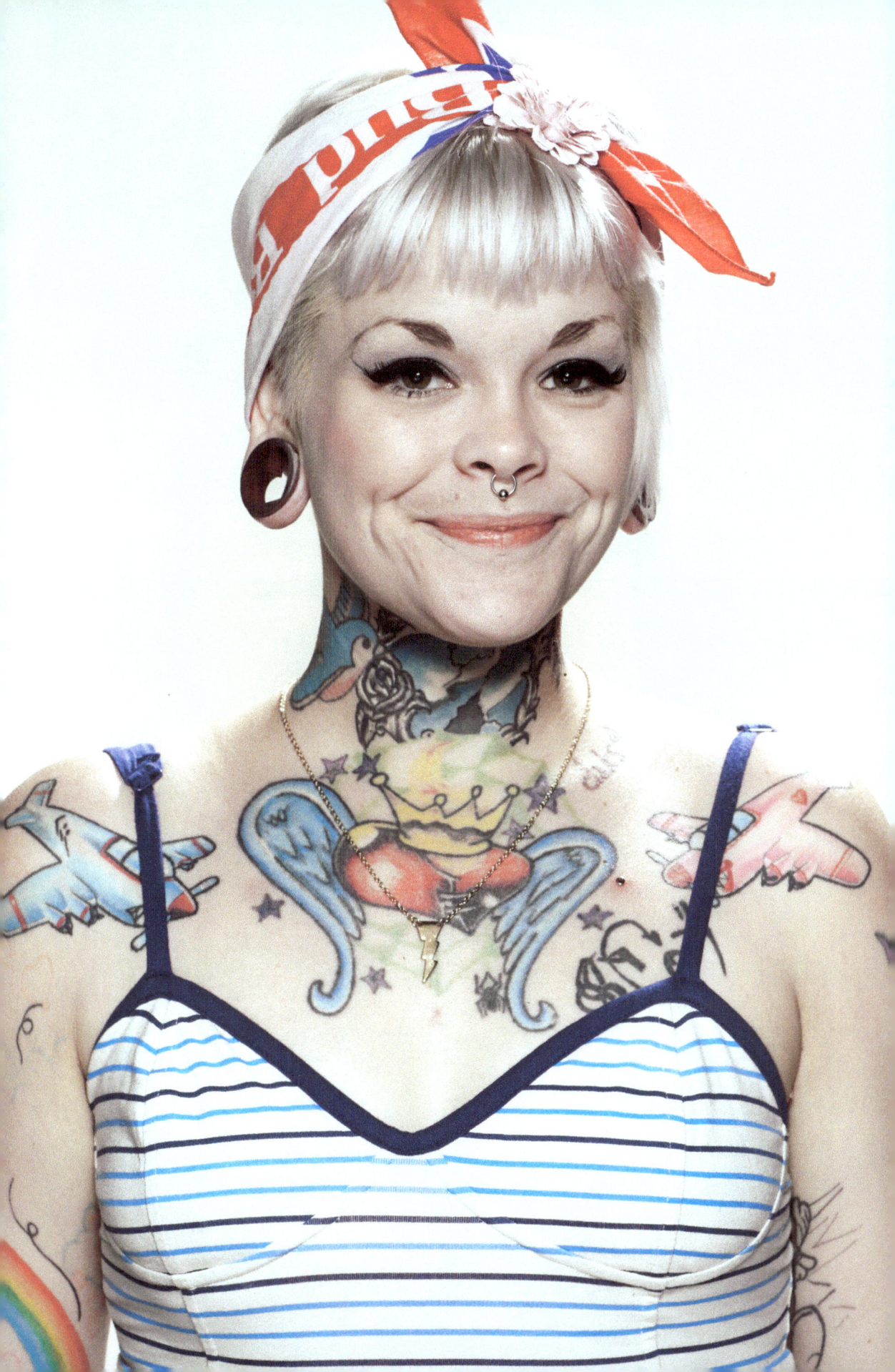

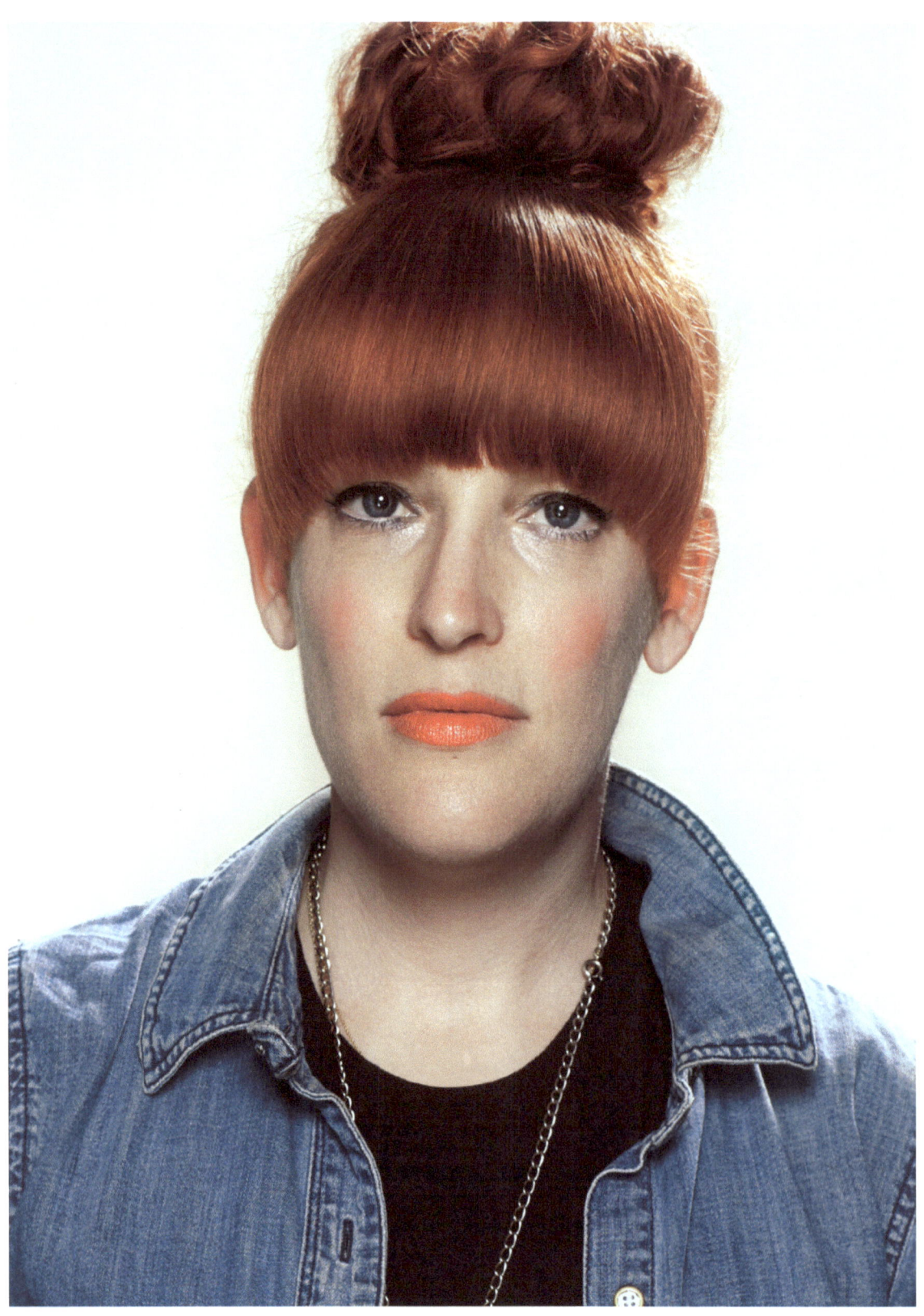

Amanda Barstow

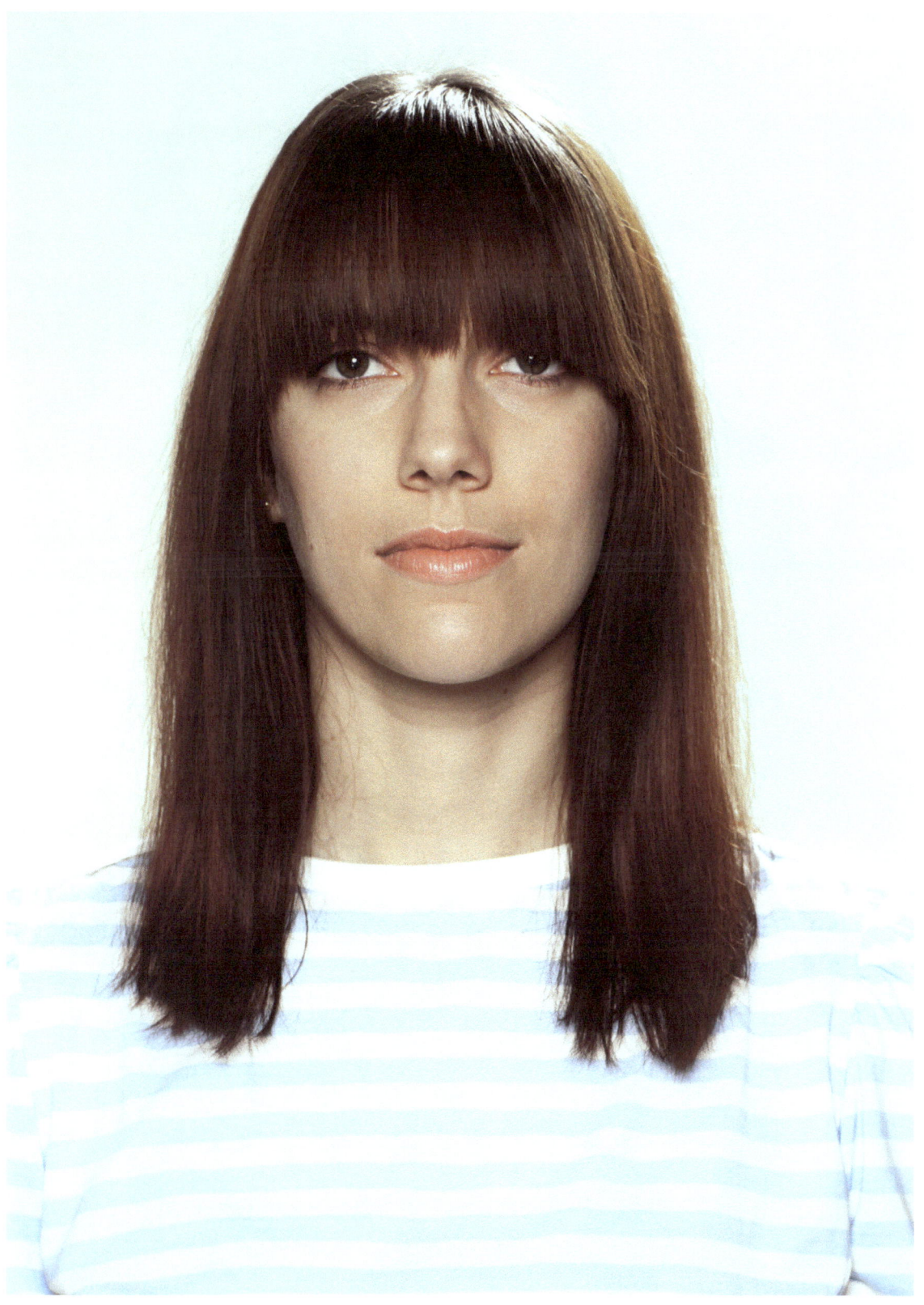

Teresa Nichta

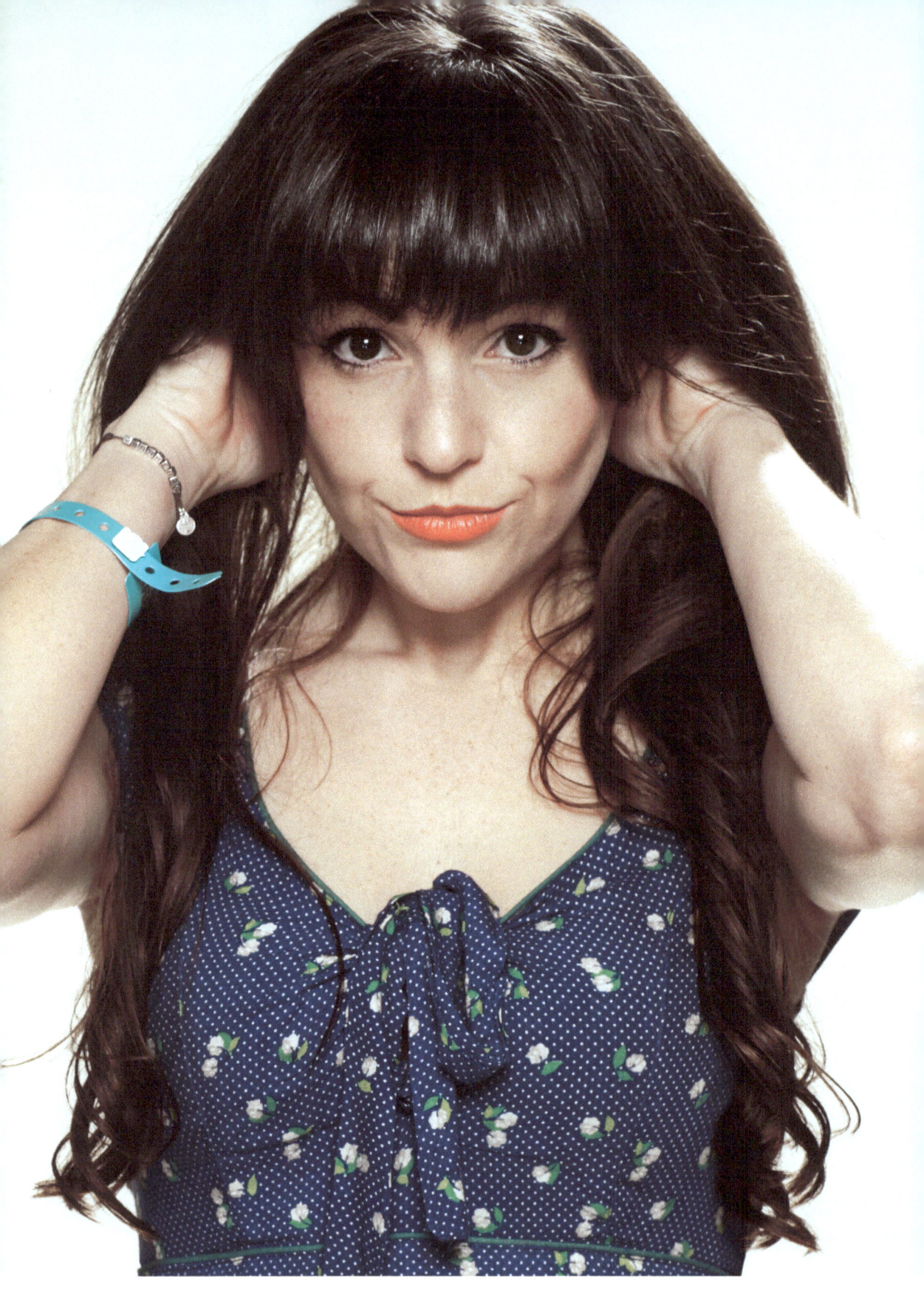

Megan J Rutherford

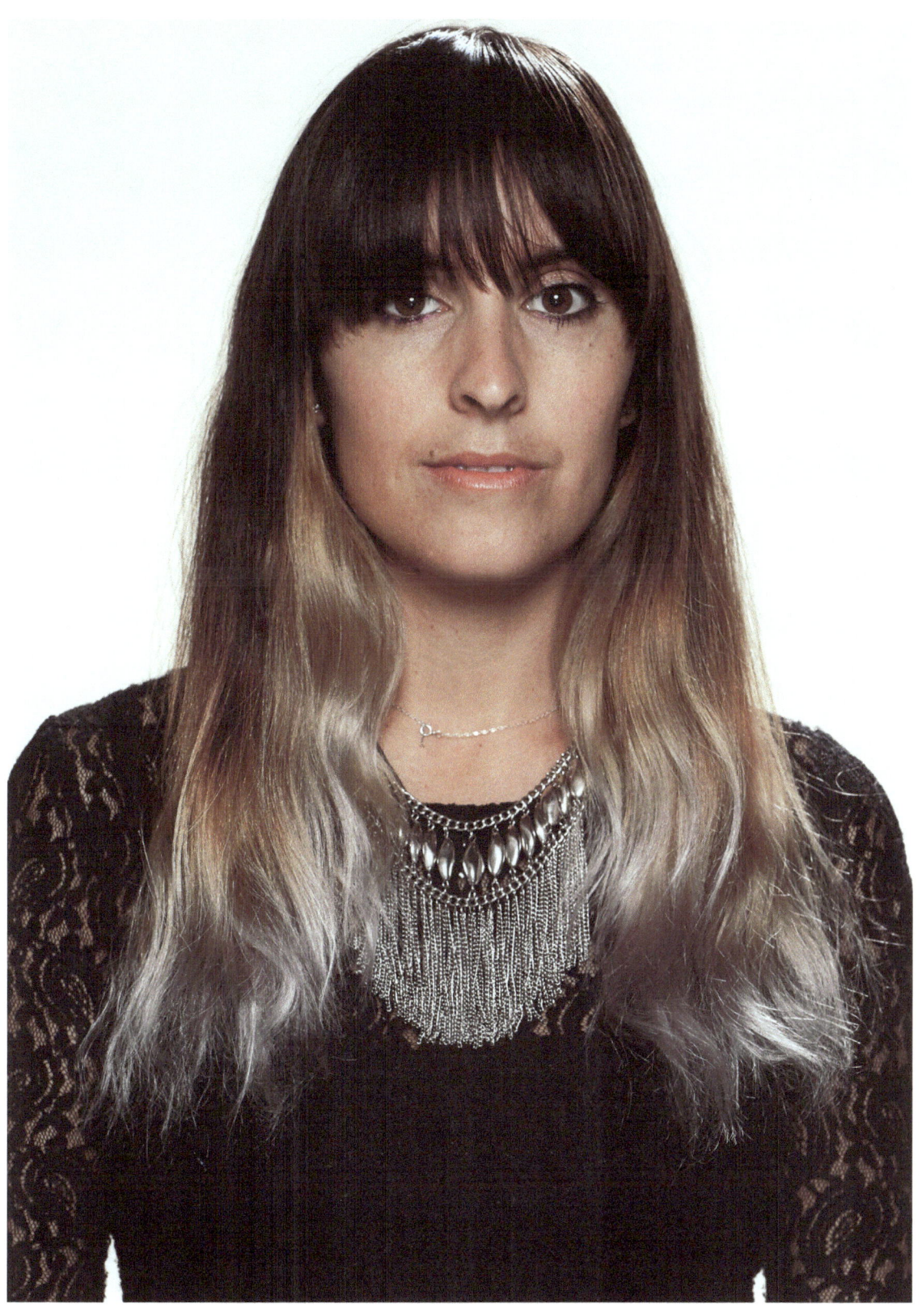

Rhiannon Atkinson-Howatt

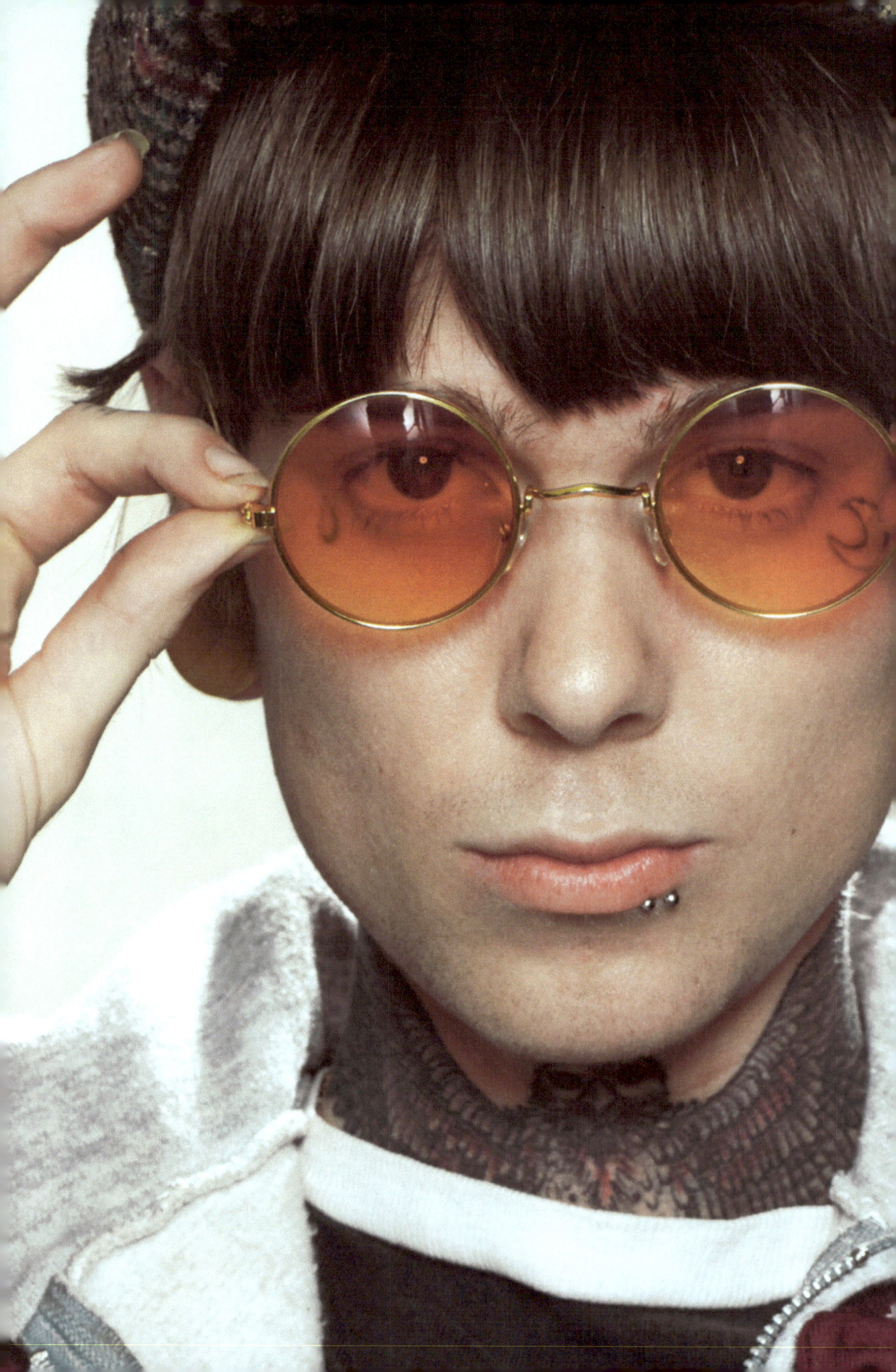

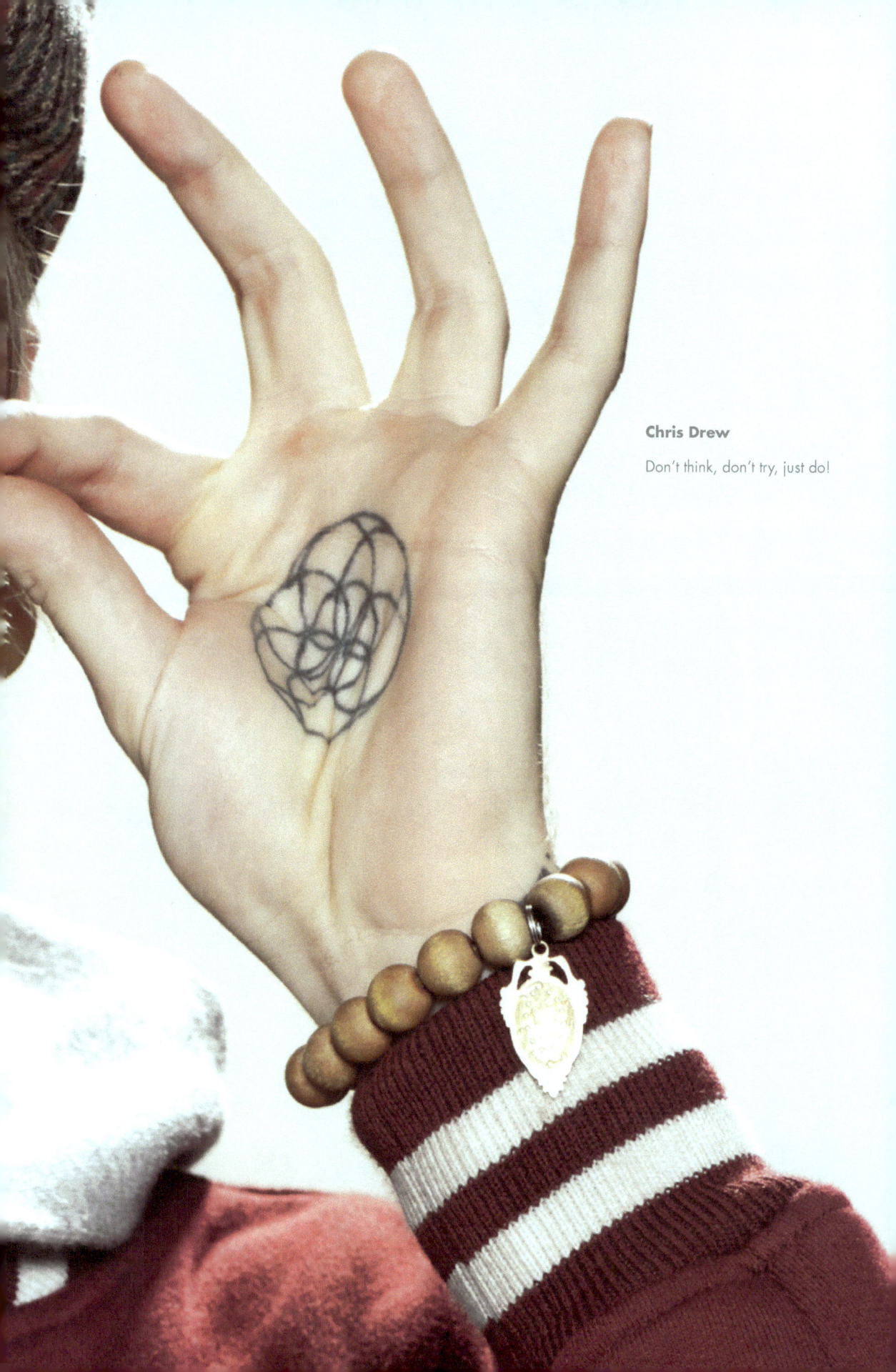

Chris Drew

Don't think, don't try, just do!

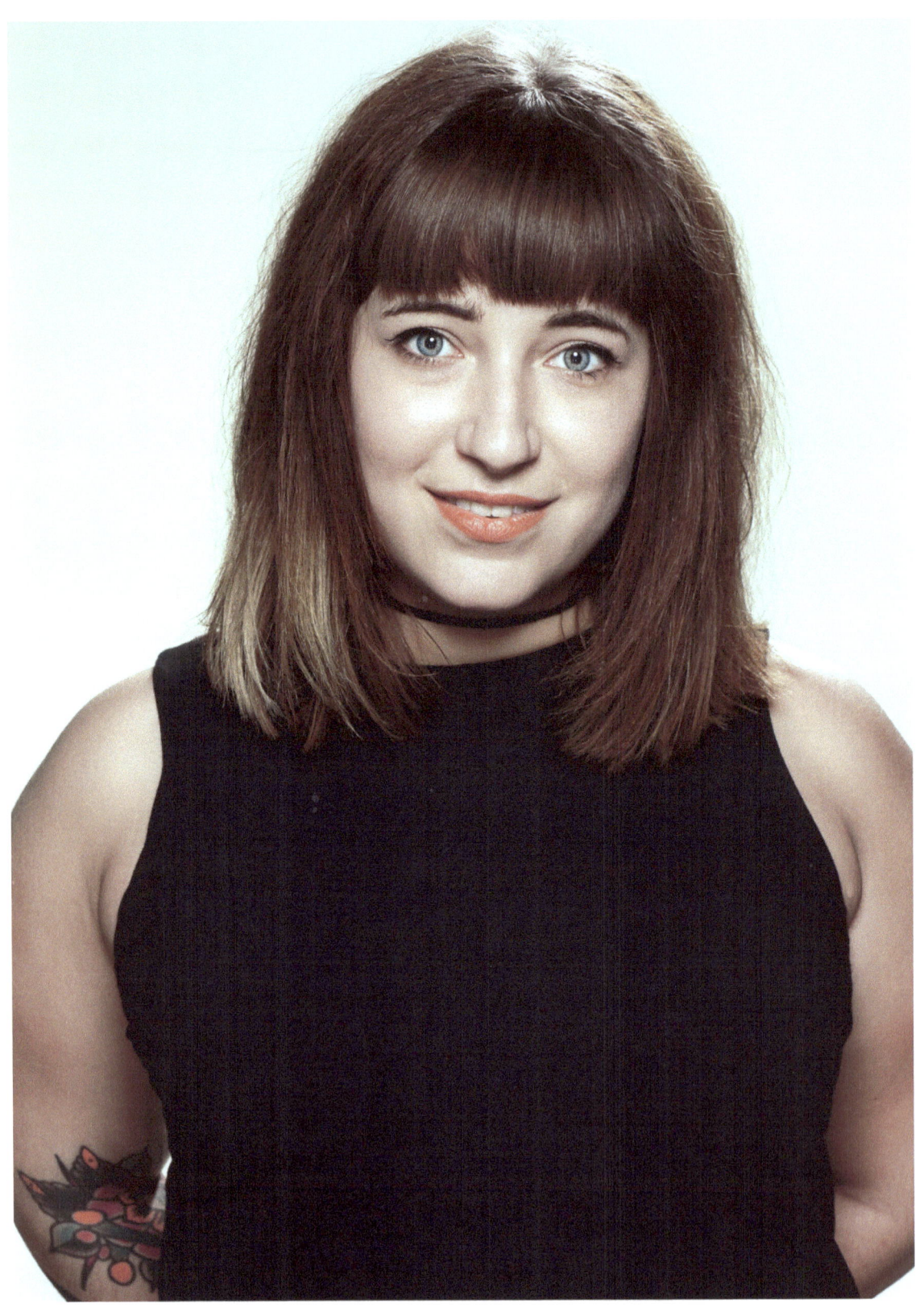

Sarah Elise Dominguez

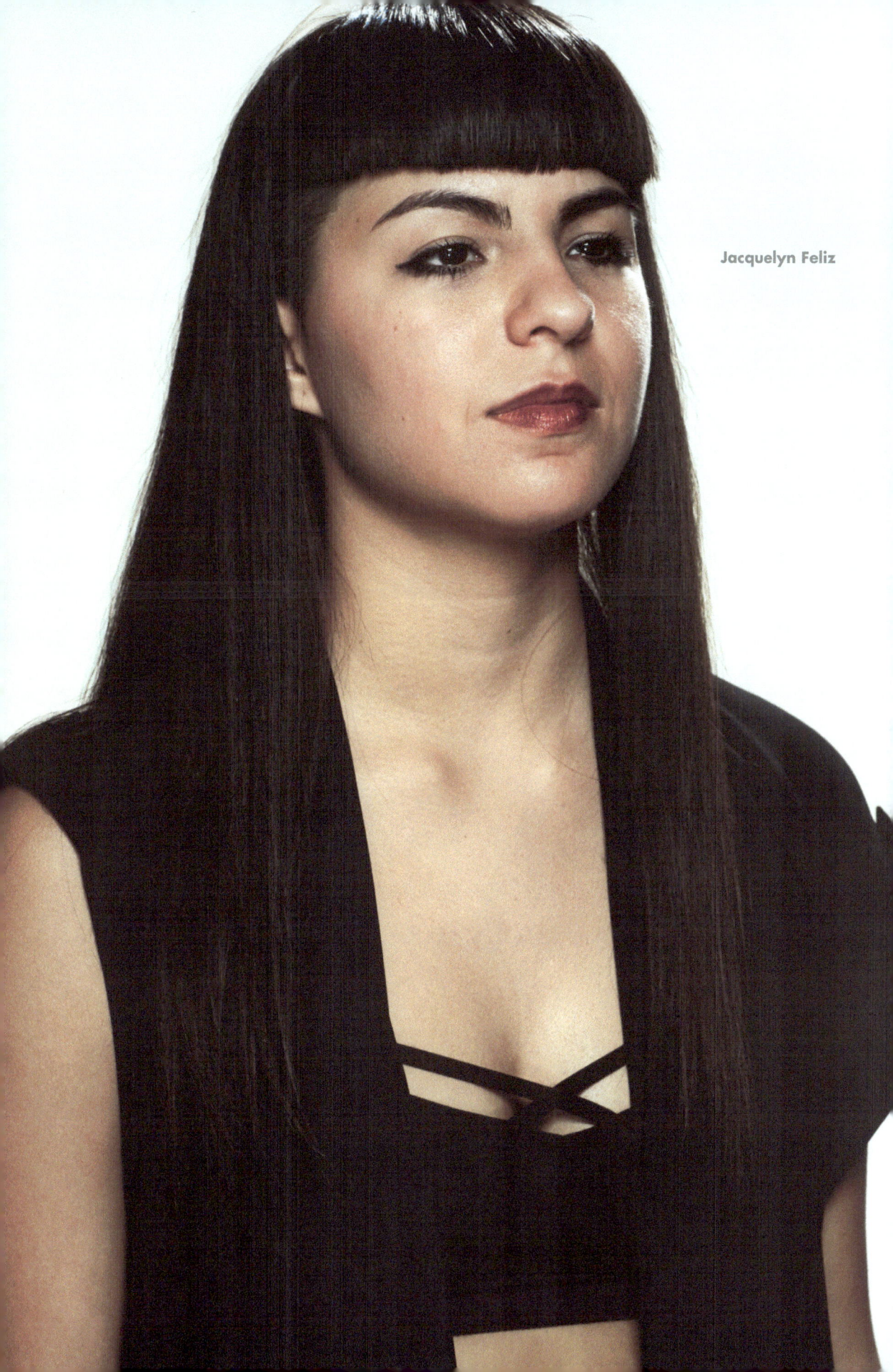

Jacquelyn Feliz

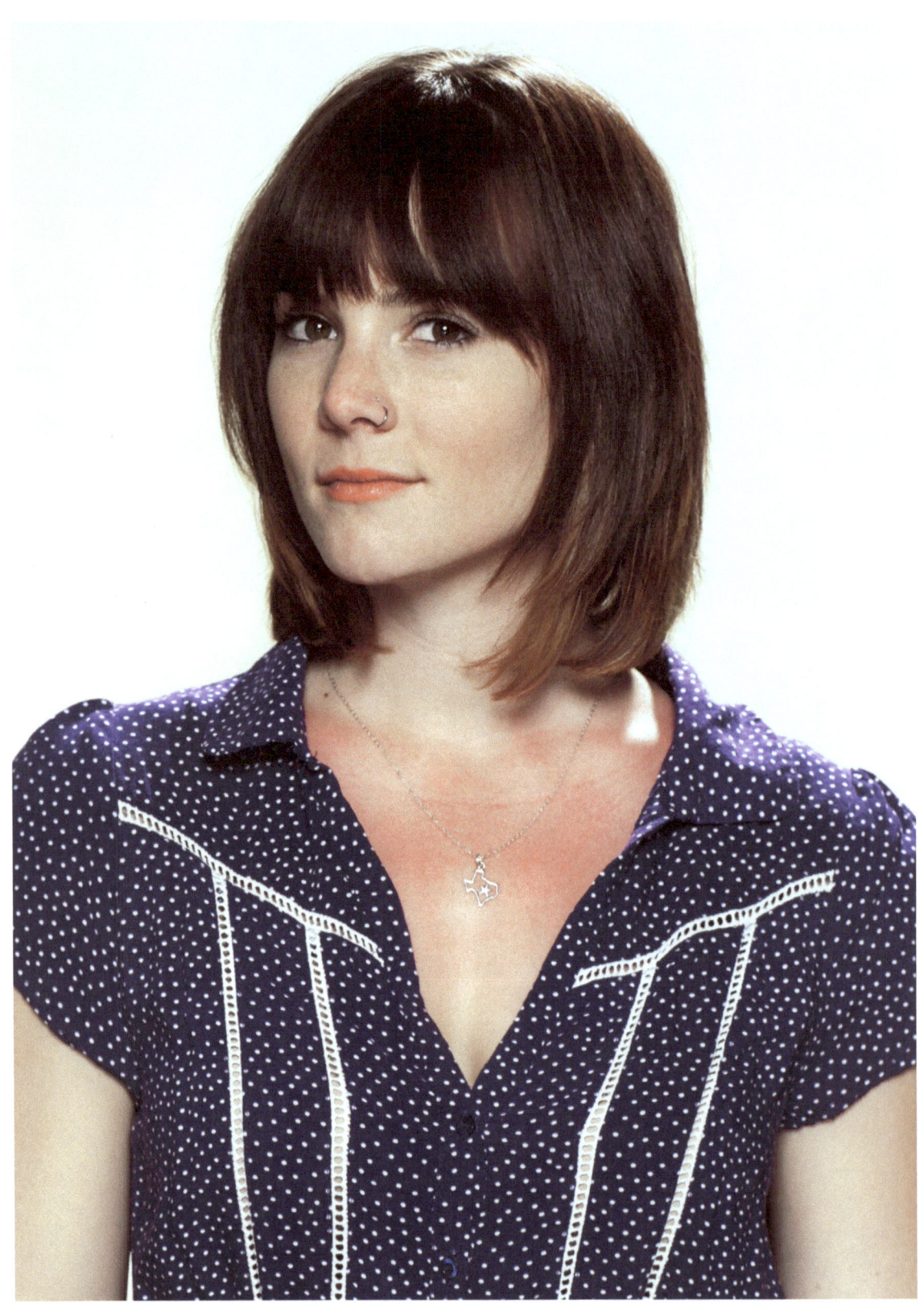

Kimberly Barrow

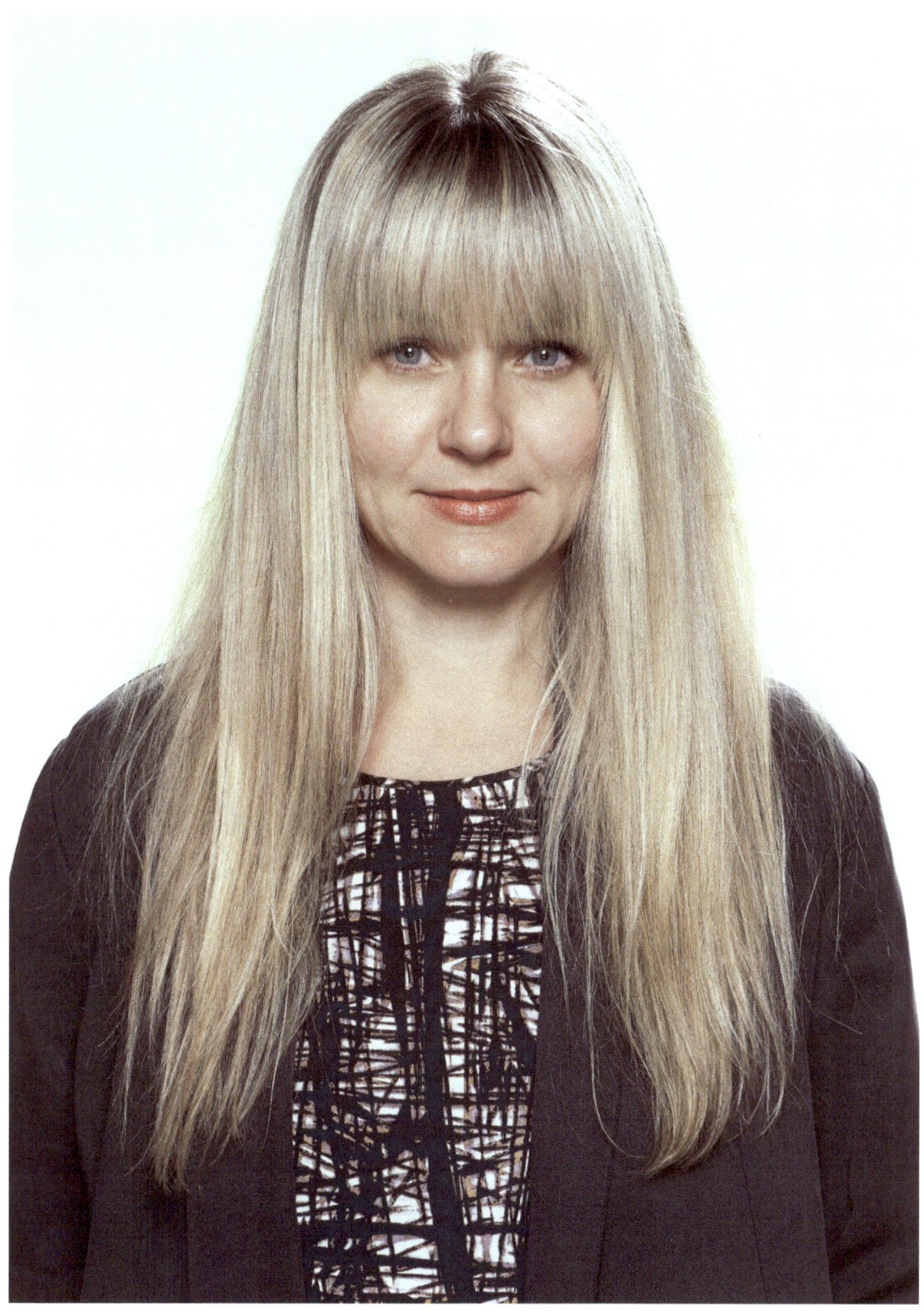

Kelly Sampley

Kelly Moore

I feel as if my hairstyle is a statement,
and as a teacher, I try to trick the kids
into thinking I'm cool!

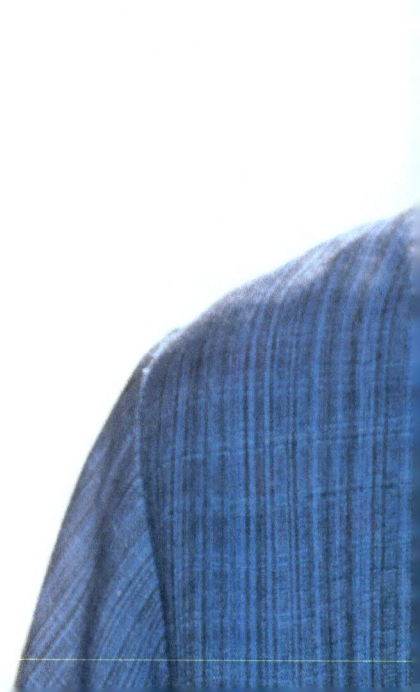

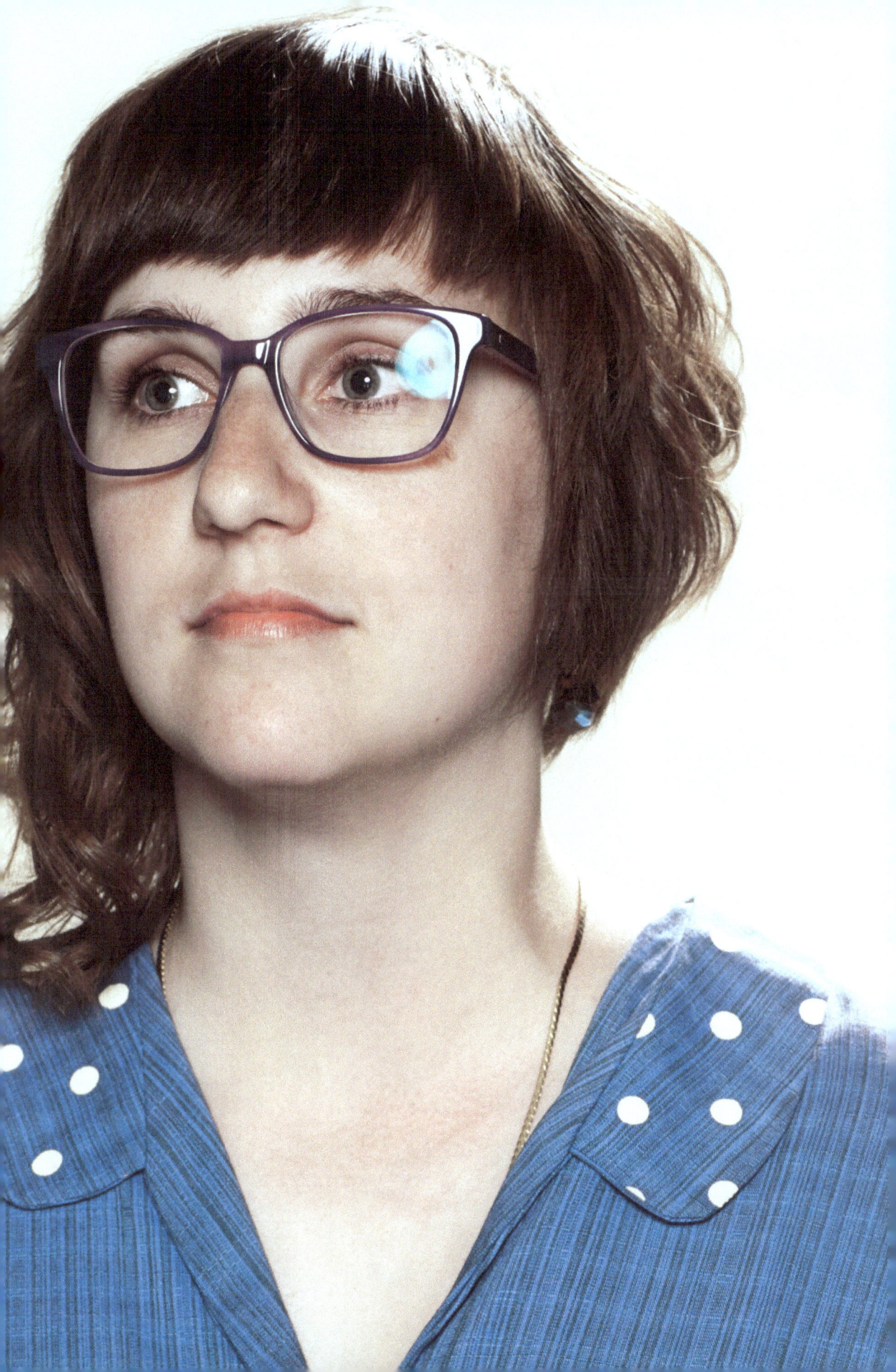

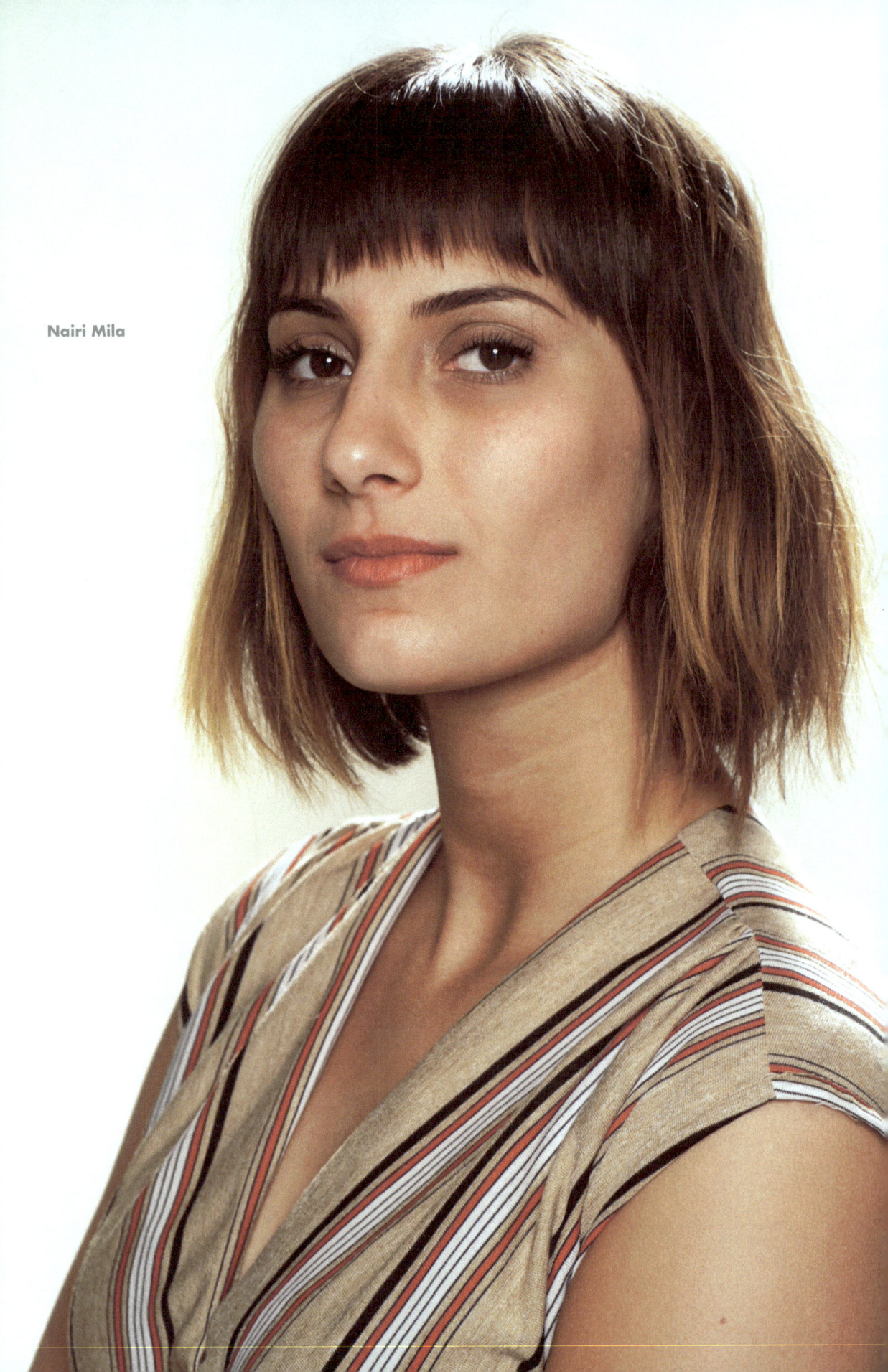

Nairi Mila

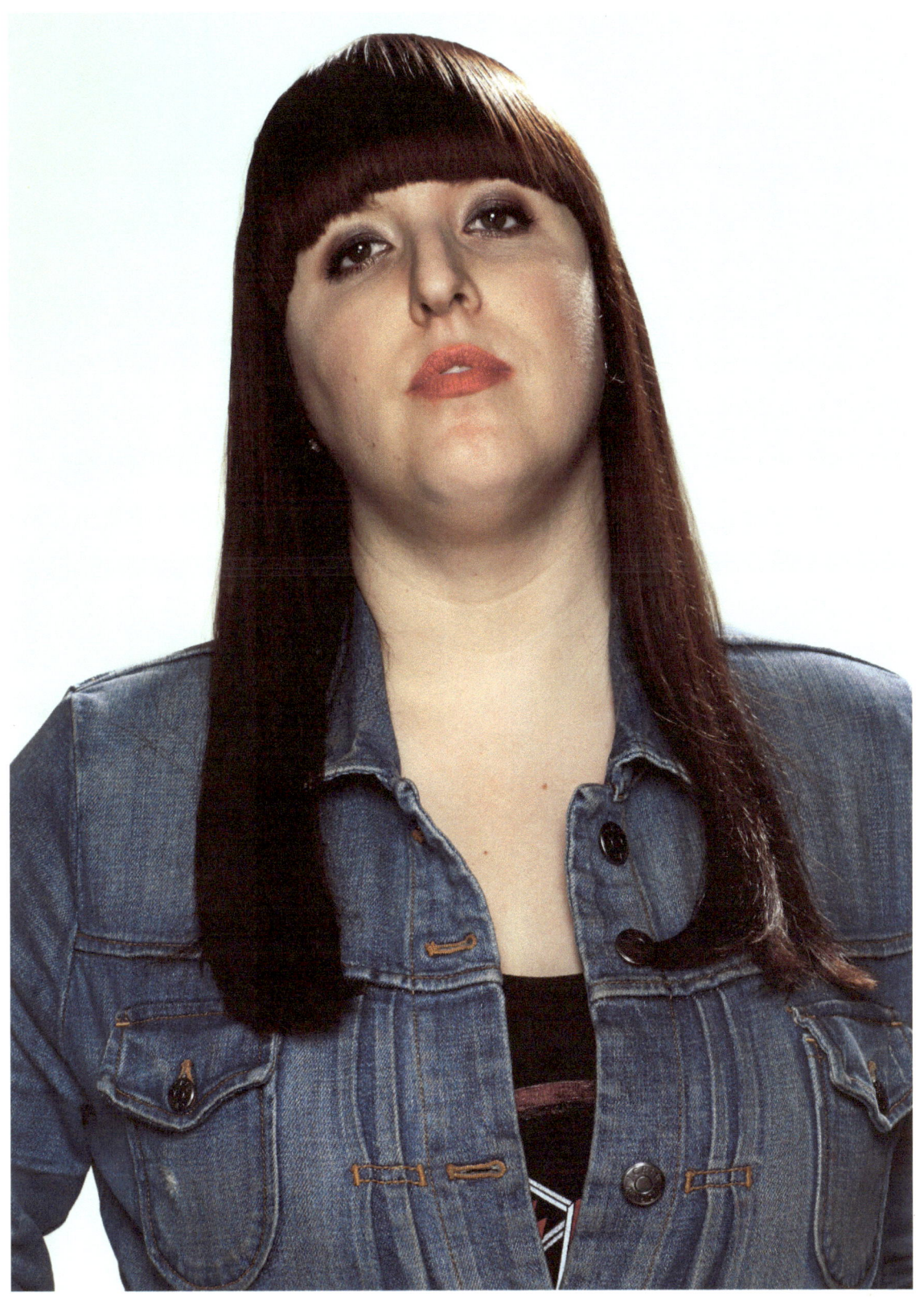

Tamara Lott

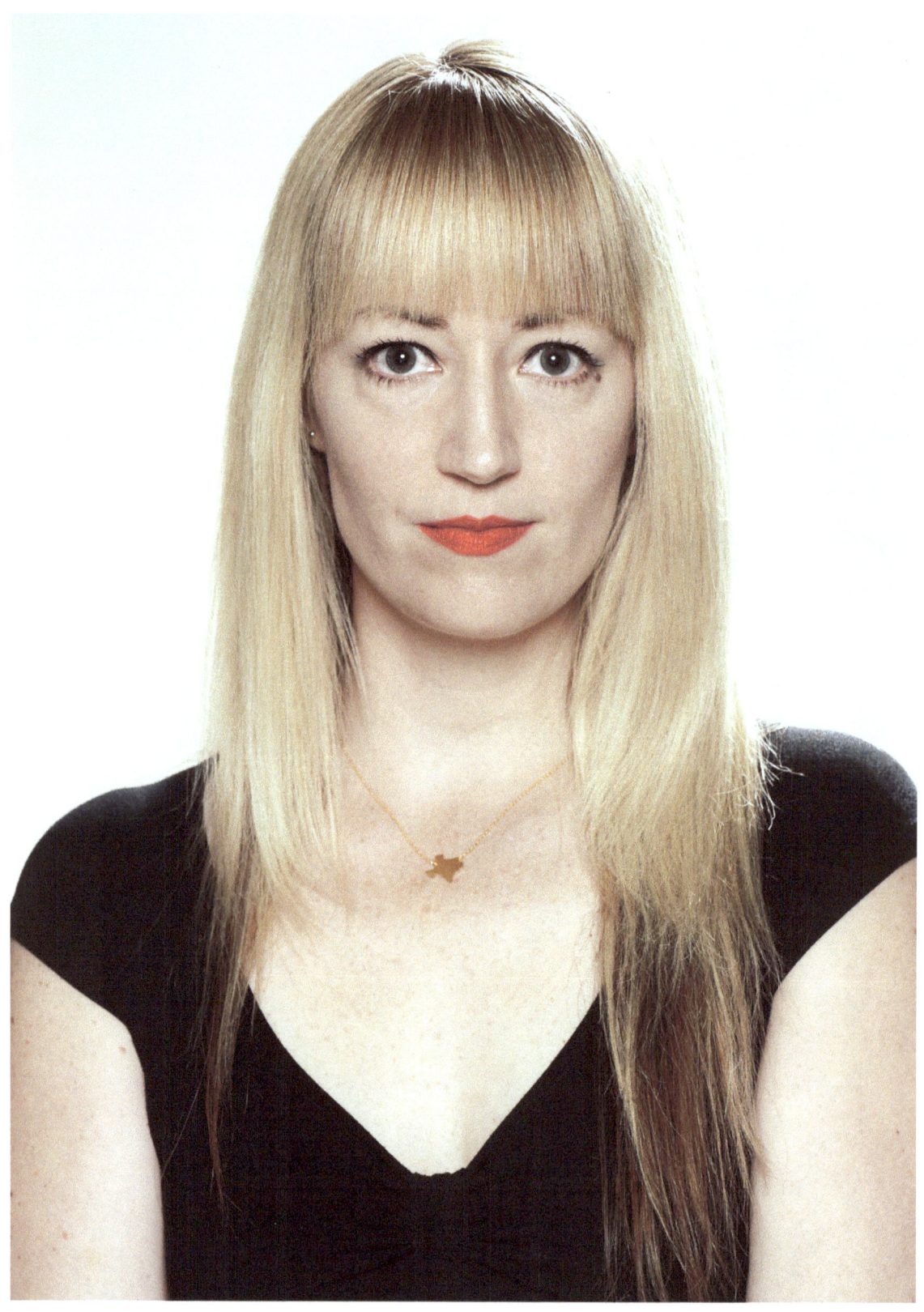

Liz Lock

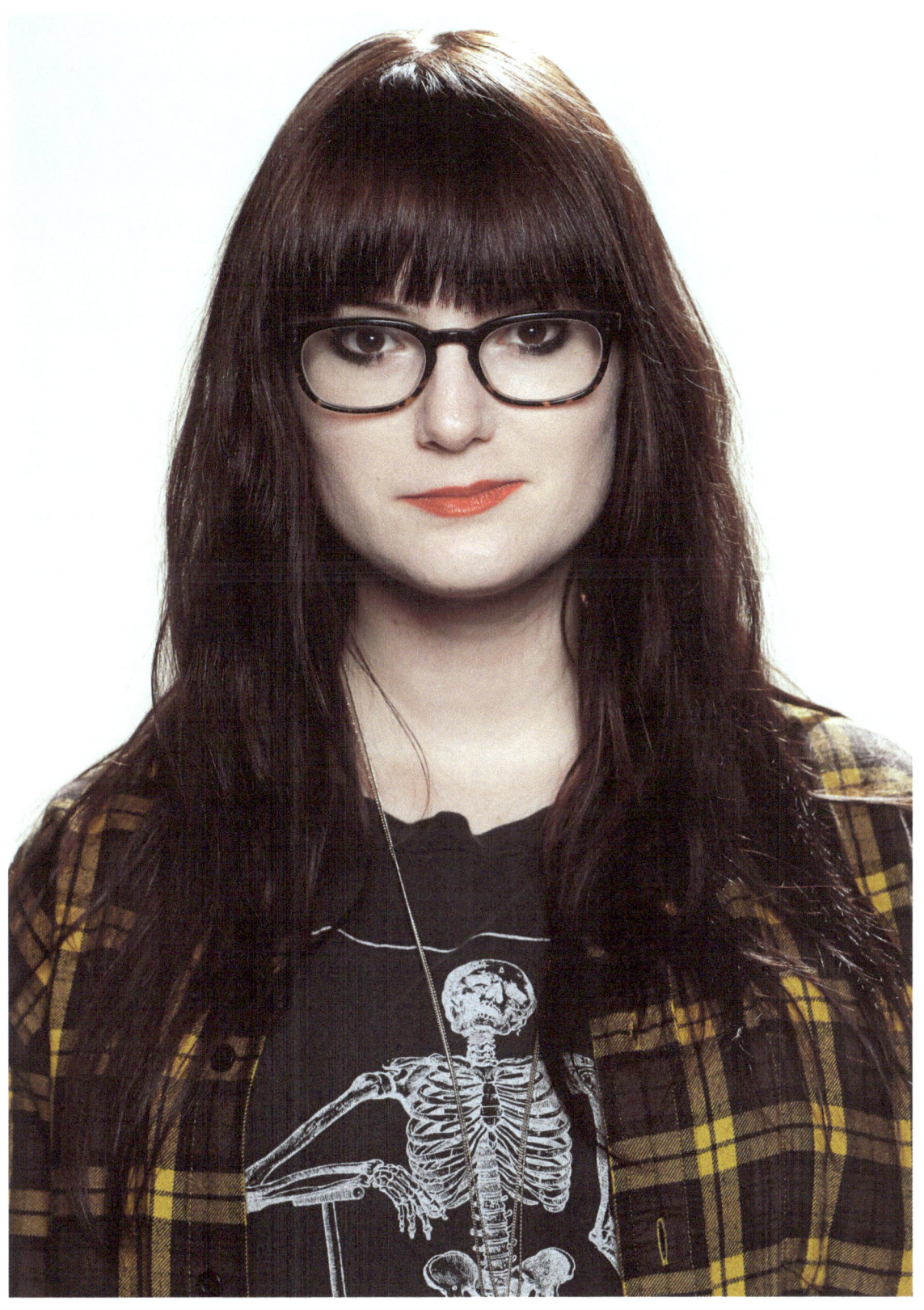

Stephanie Breijo

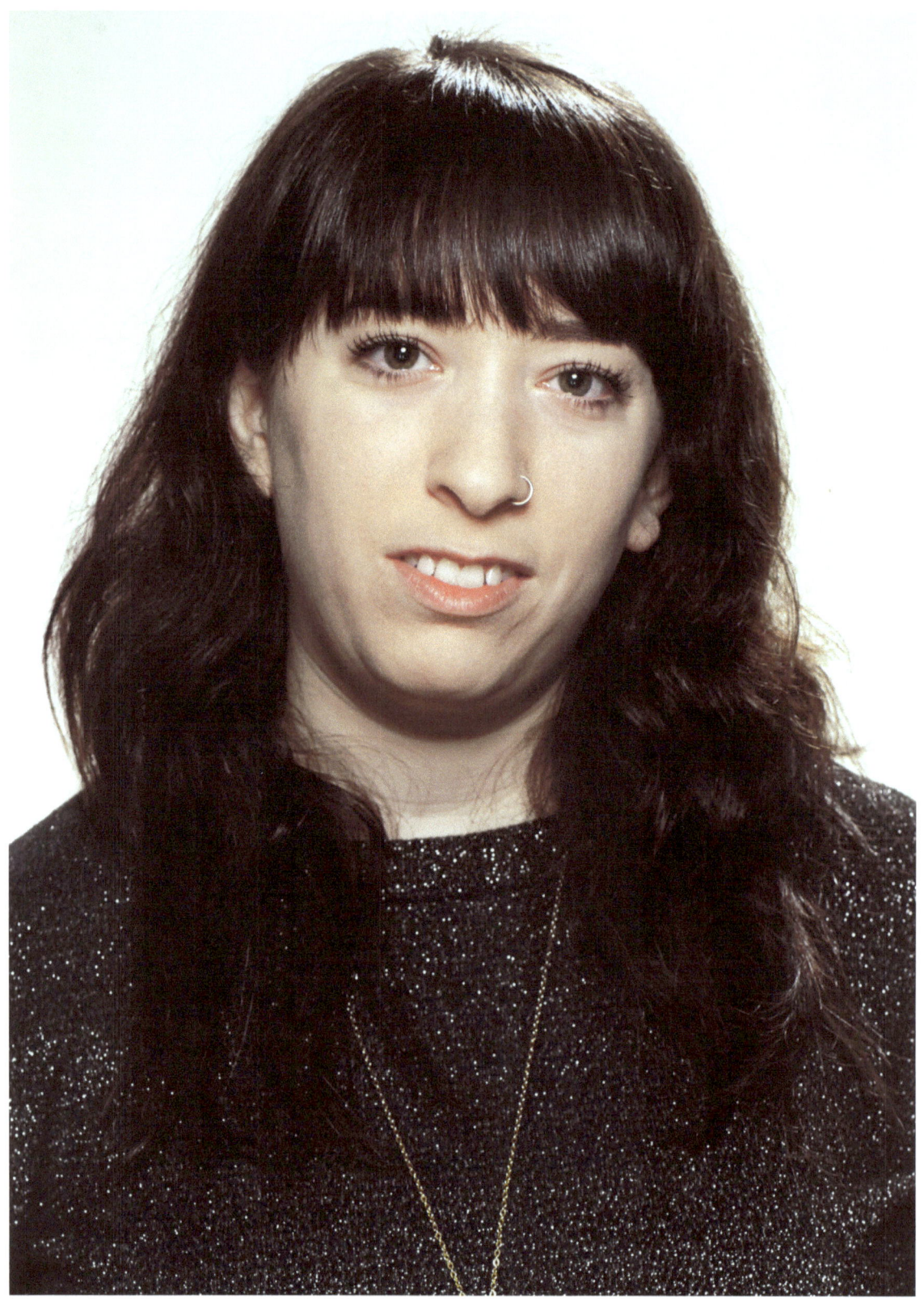

Lauren Tucker

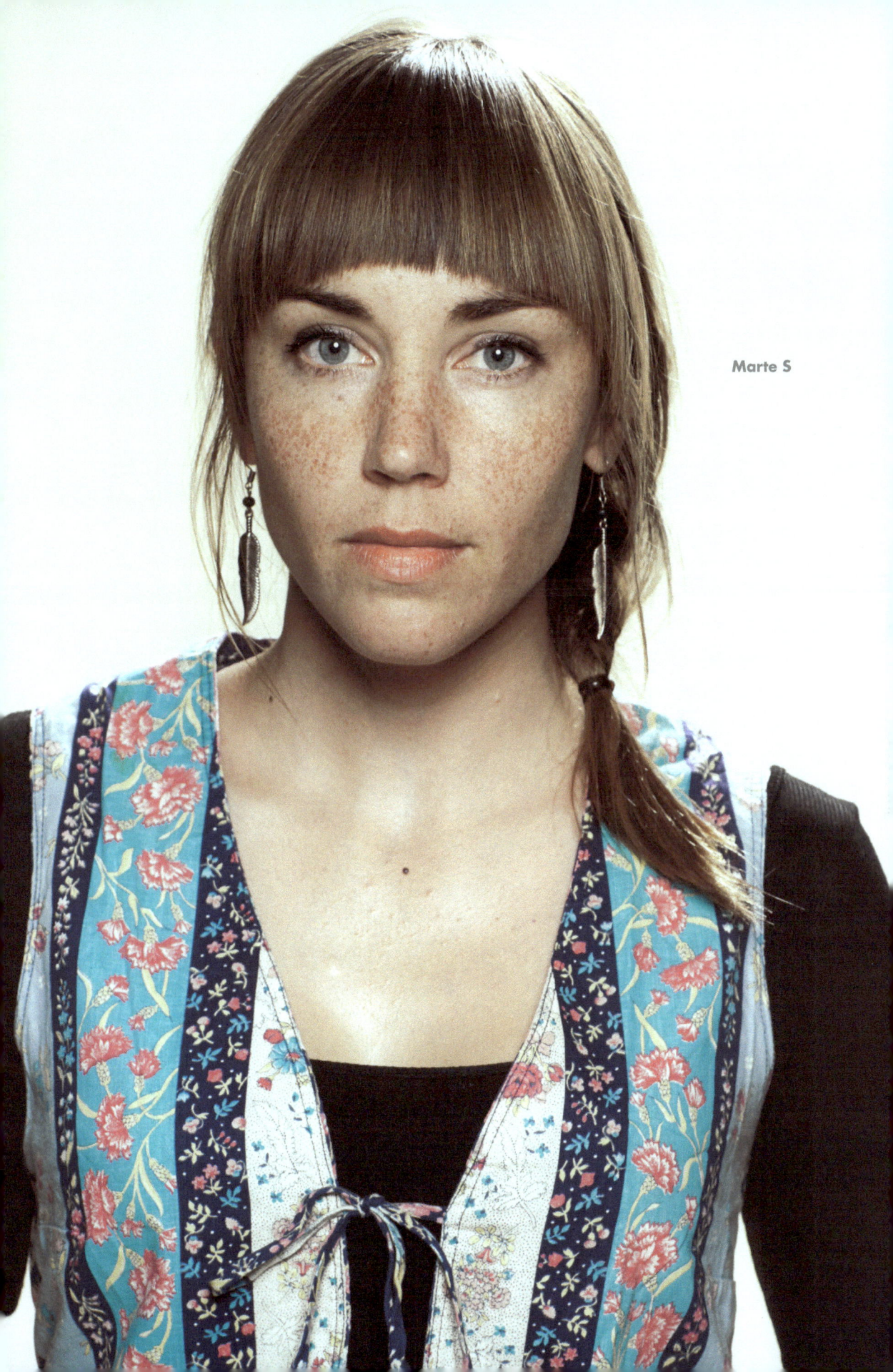

Marte S

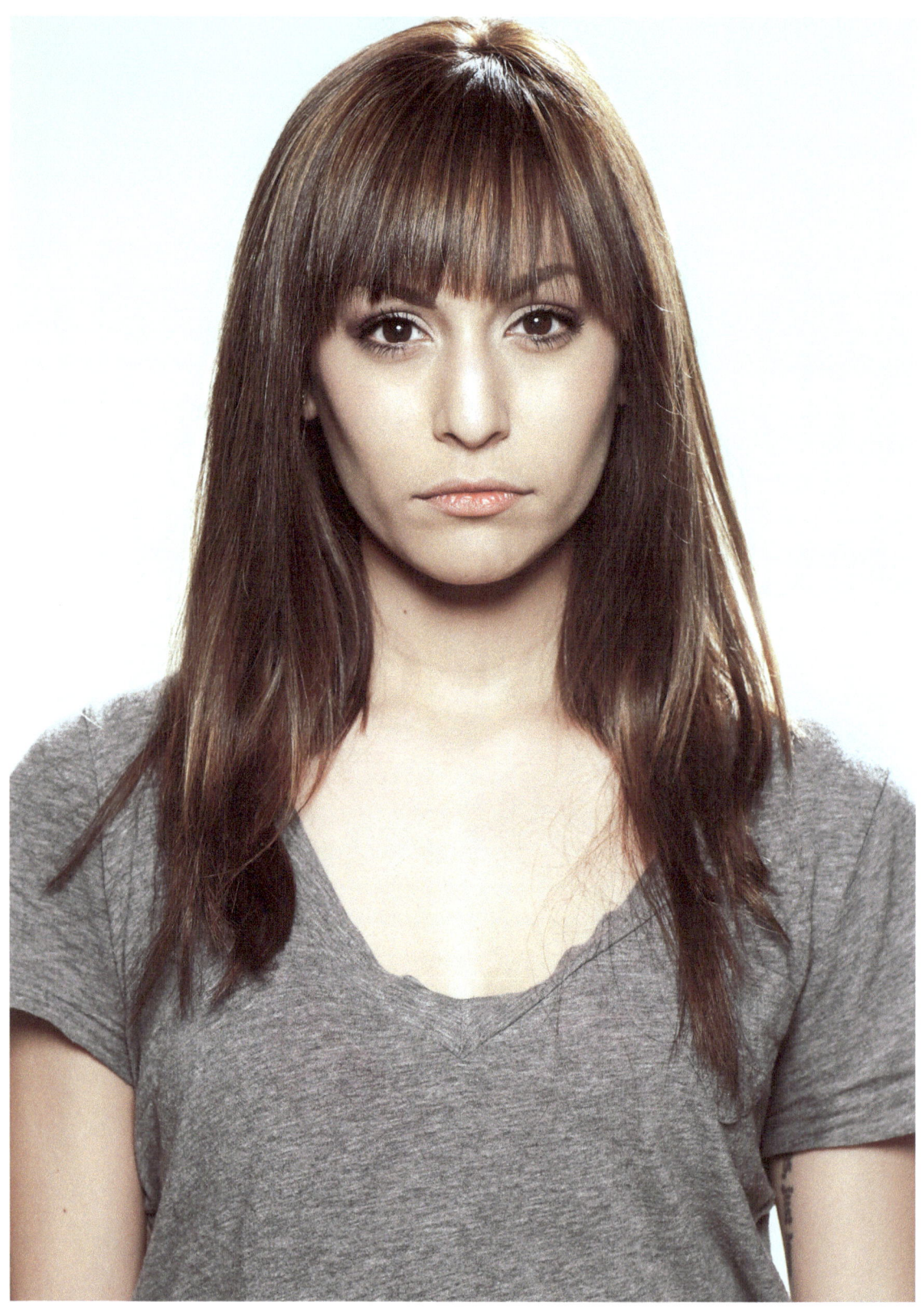

Emily Saenz

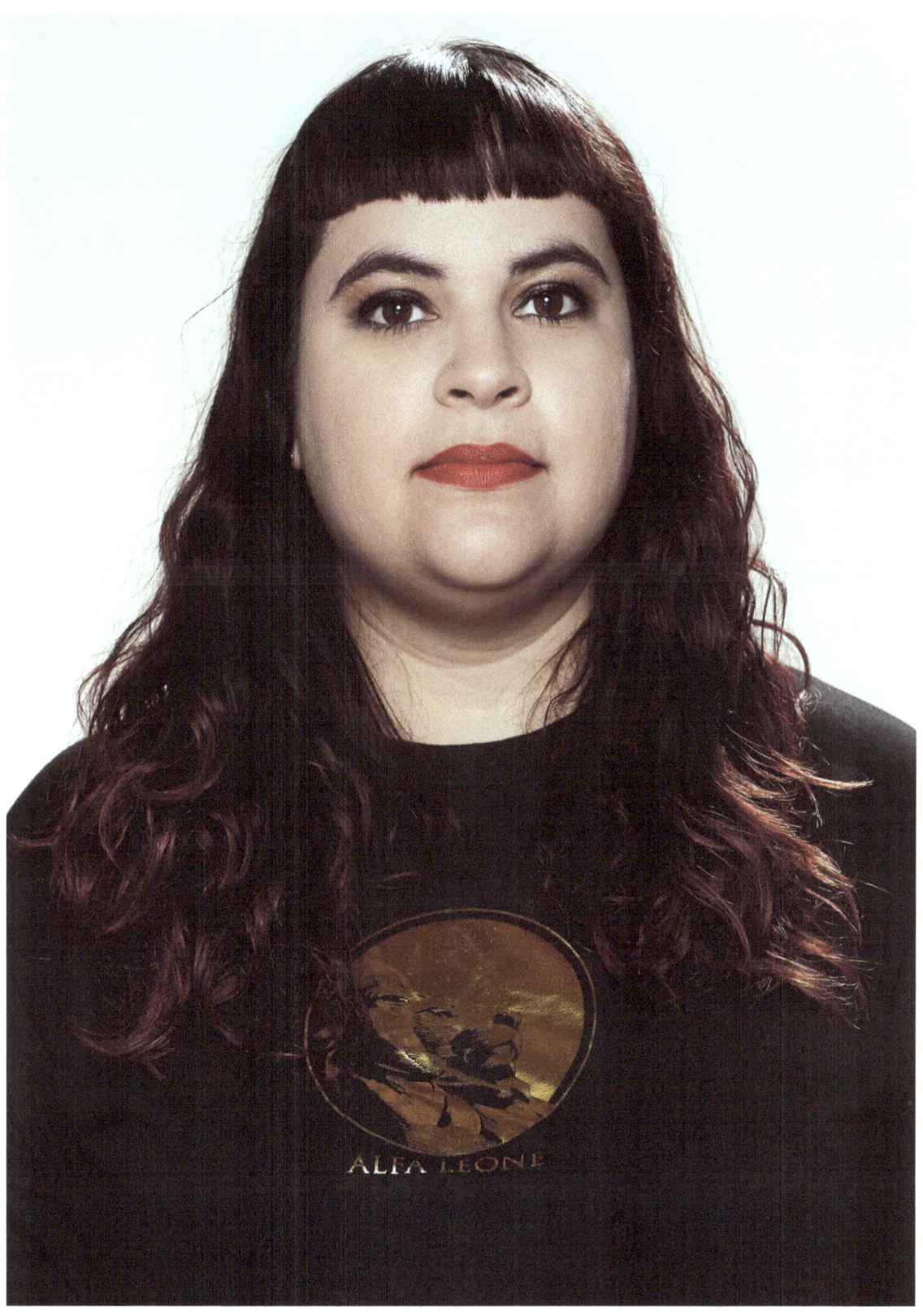

Laurie Lyons

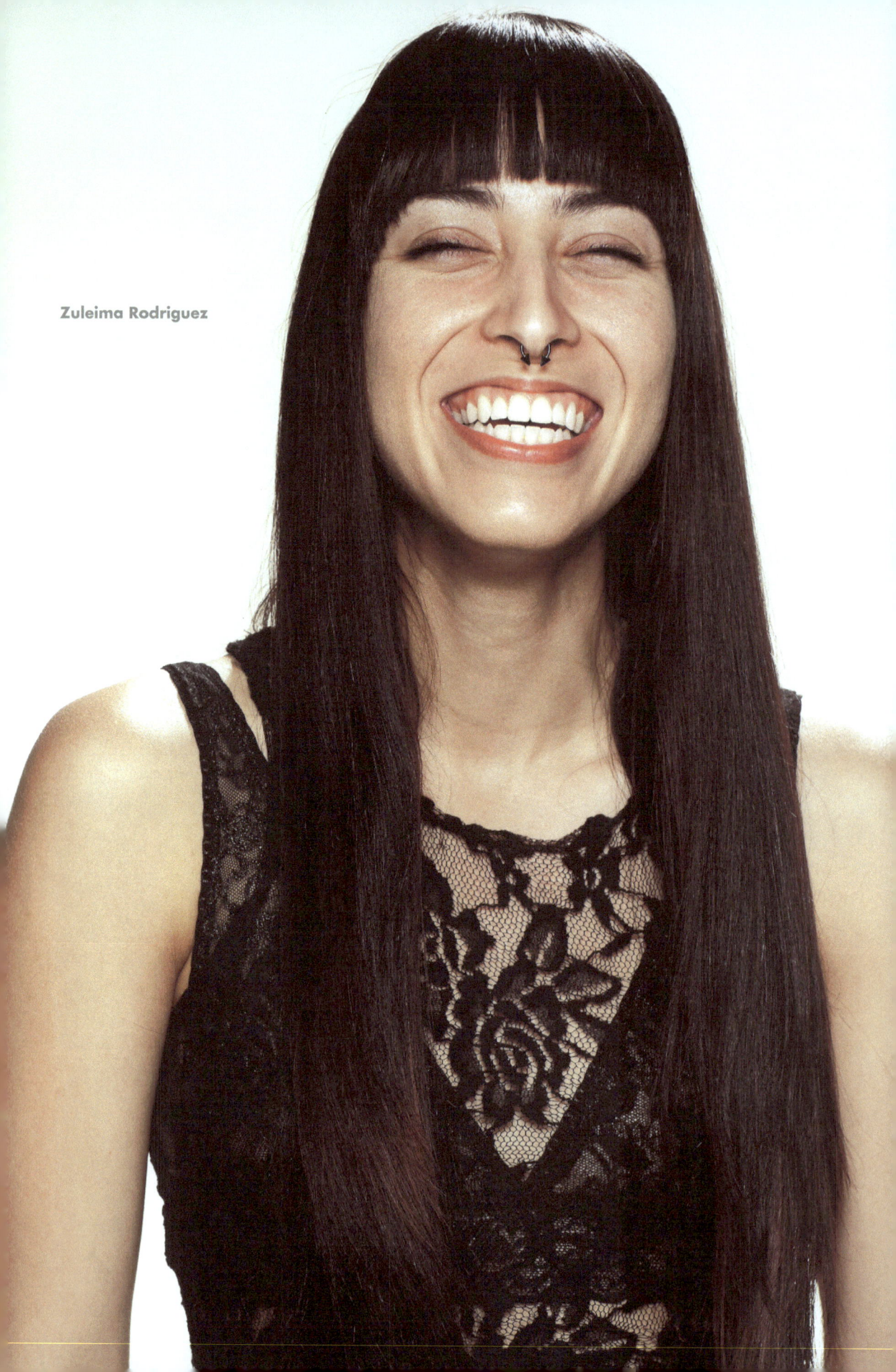

Zuleima Rodriguez

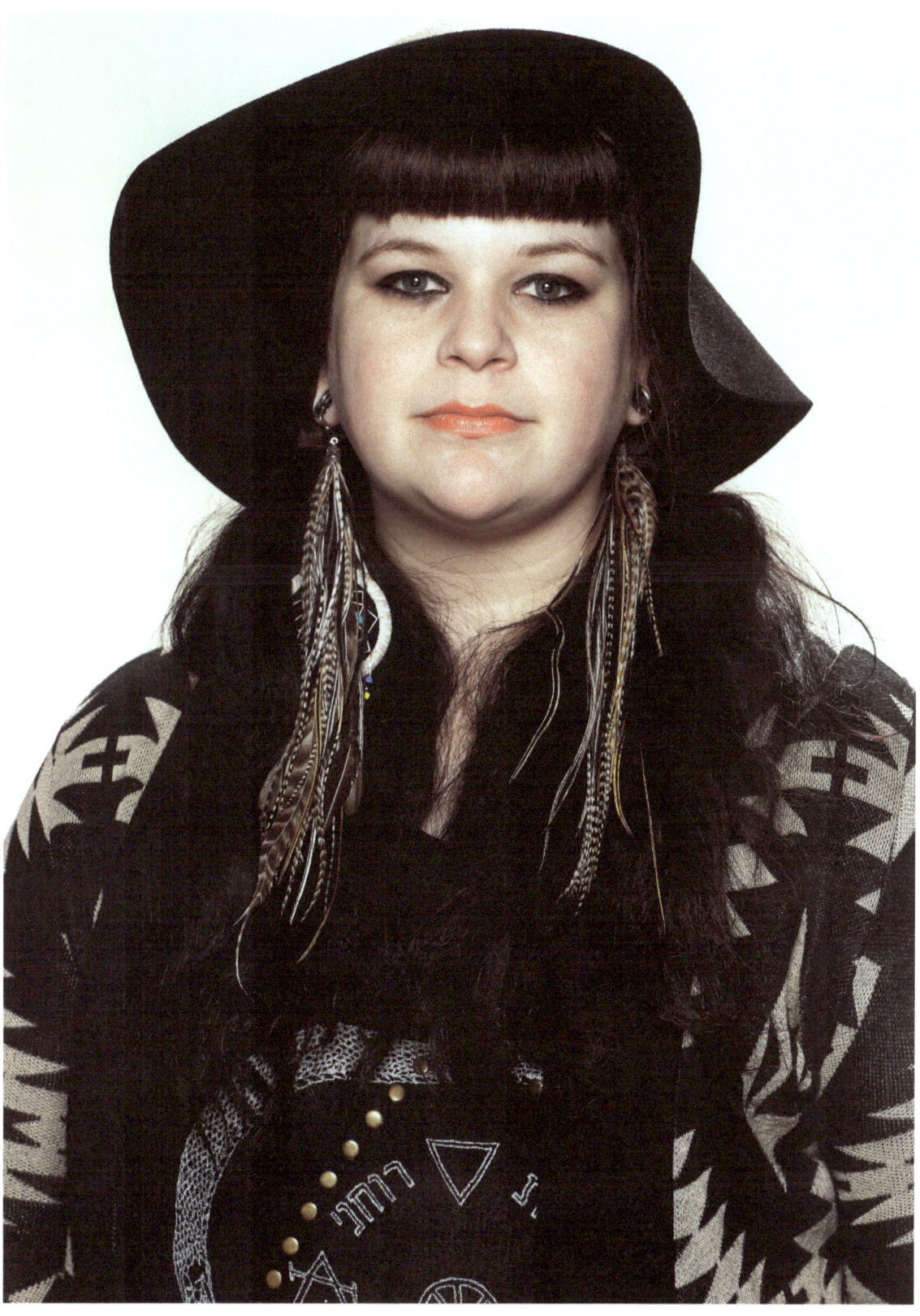

Nicole Hute

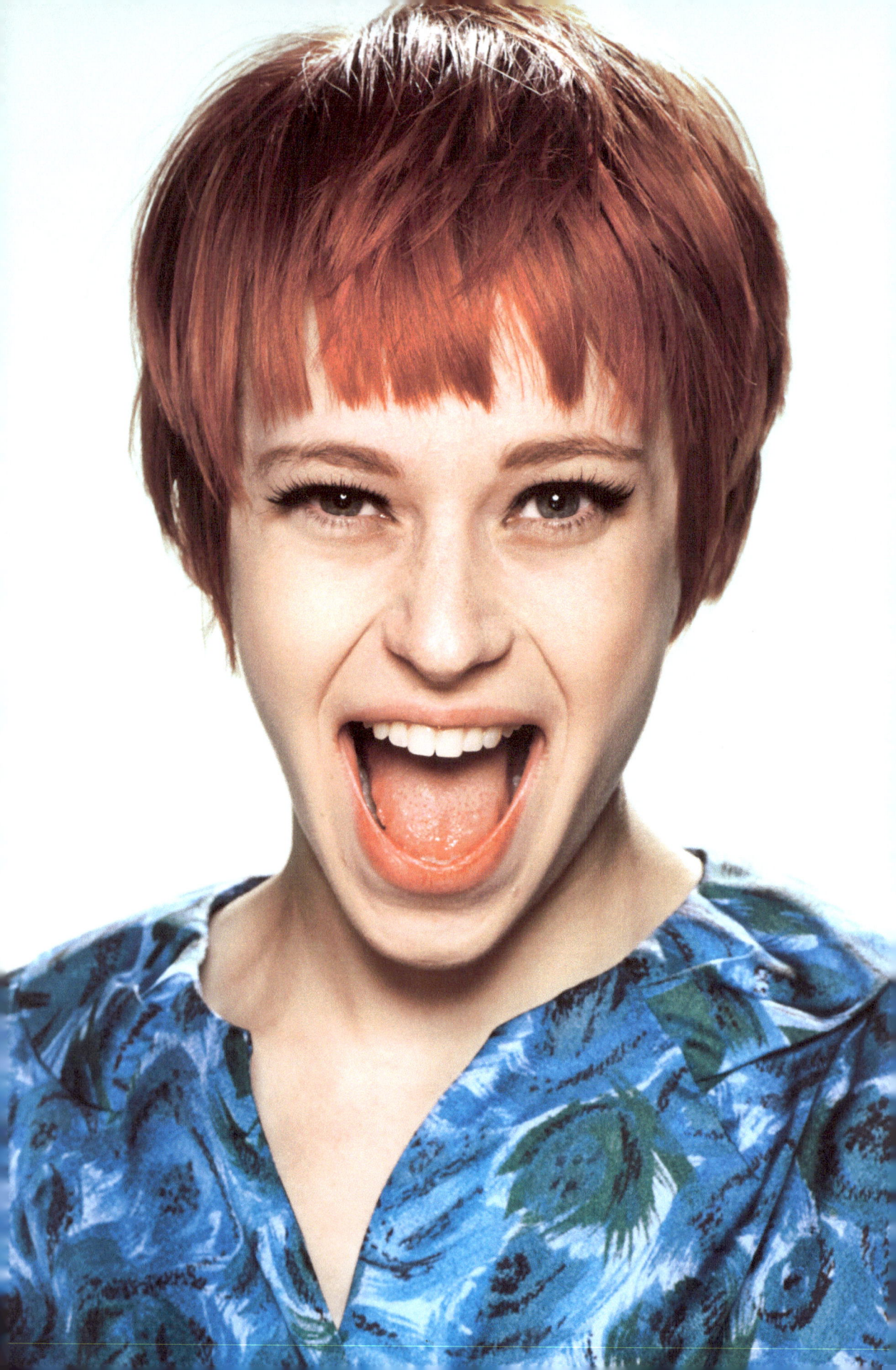

Megan Young

I have bangs because I think the way
you wear your hair completes your
look! Bangs give you the freedom to
show your quirky style, business style,
or your rocker style.

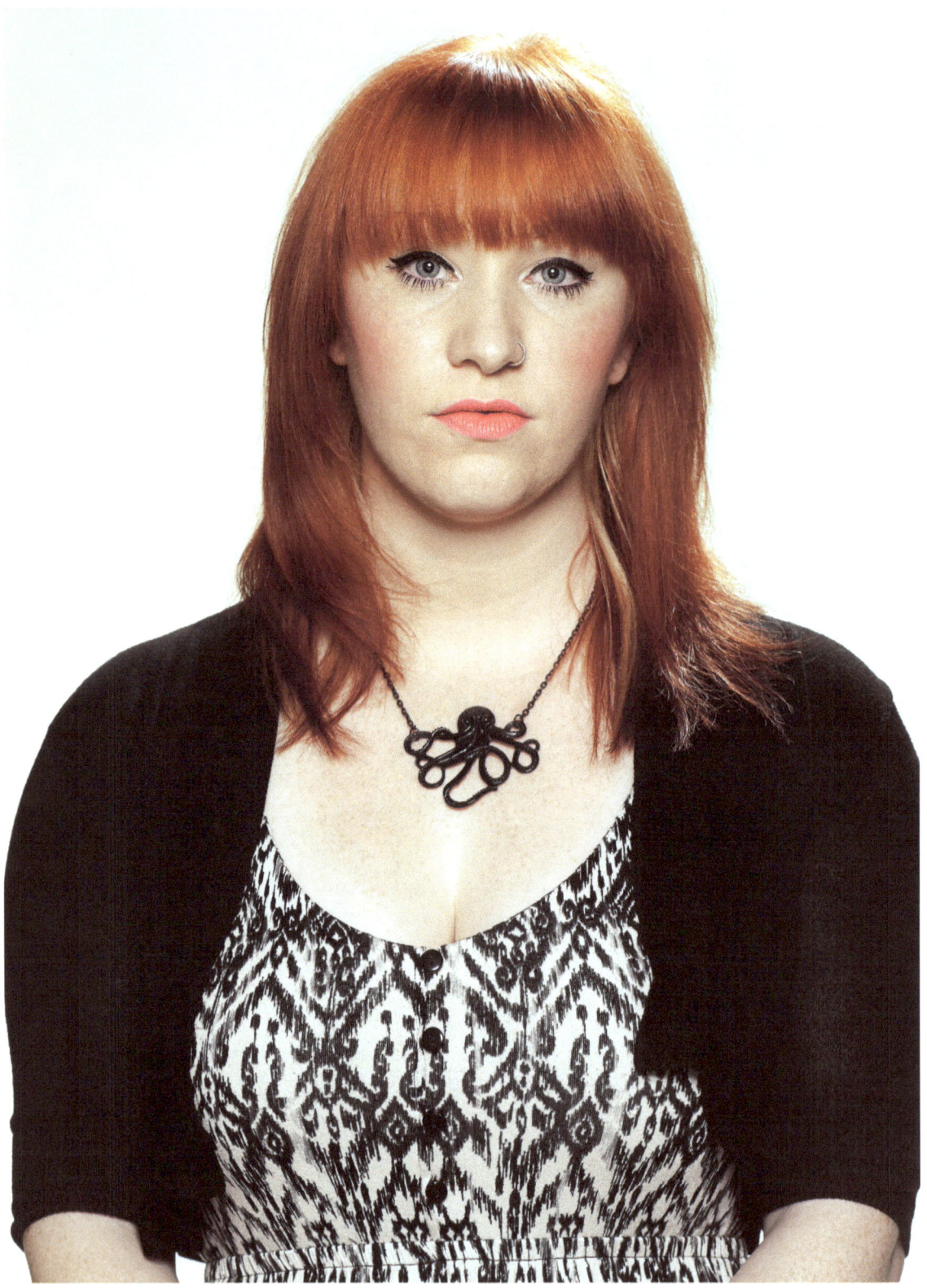

Kady Simmons

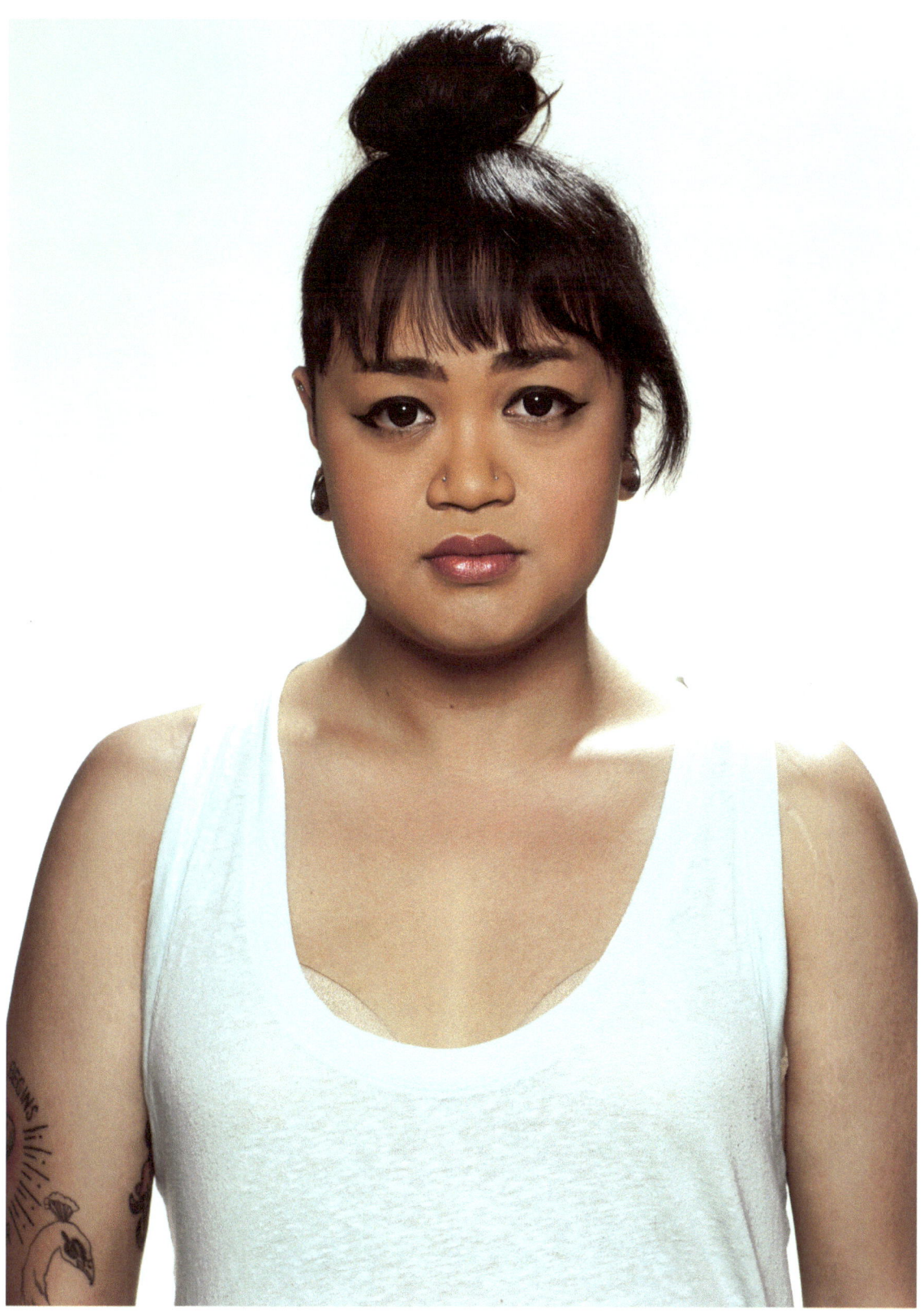

Charly Janae

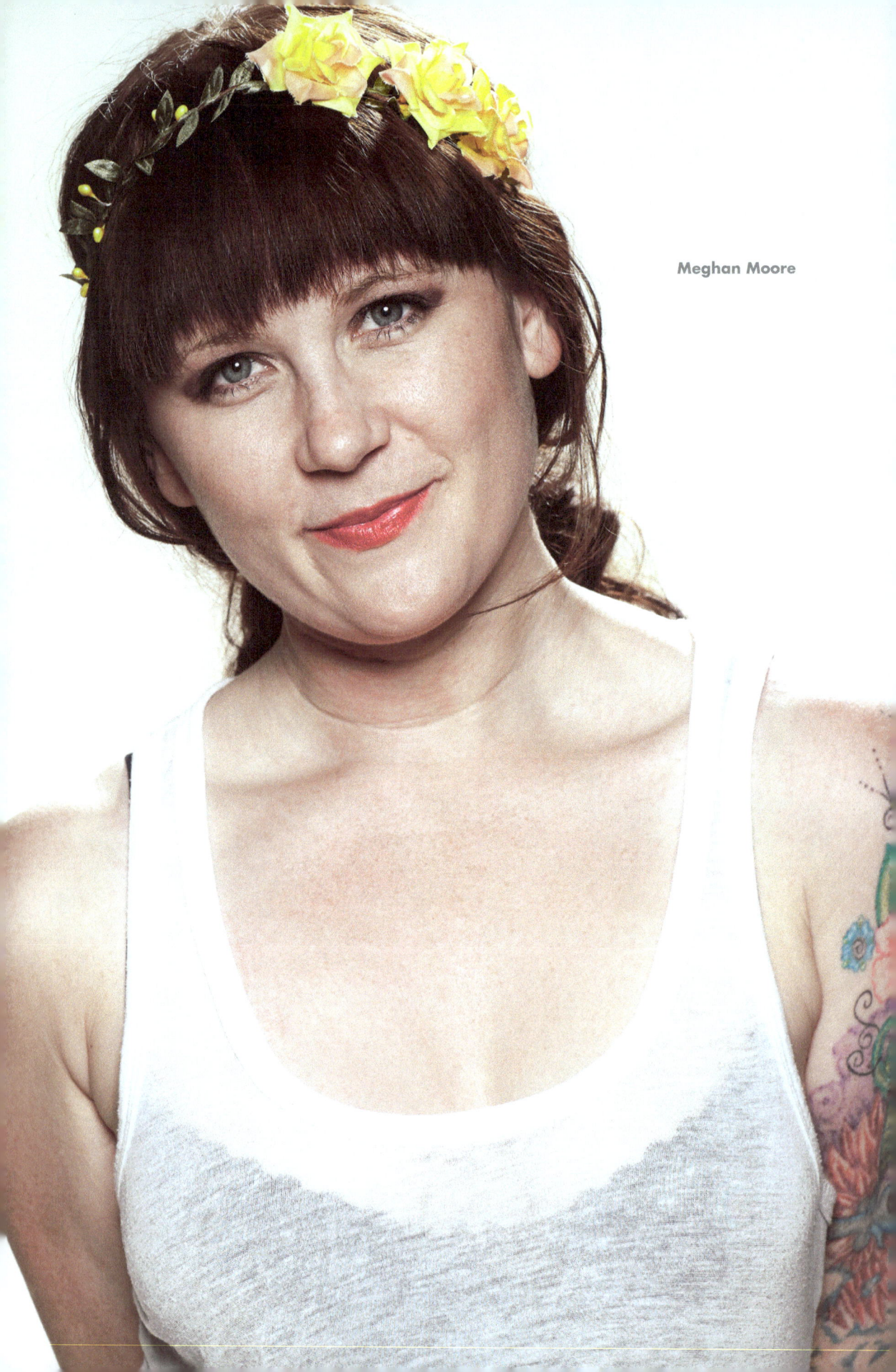
Meghan Moore

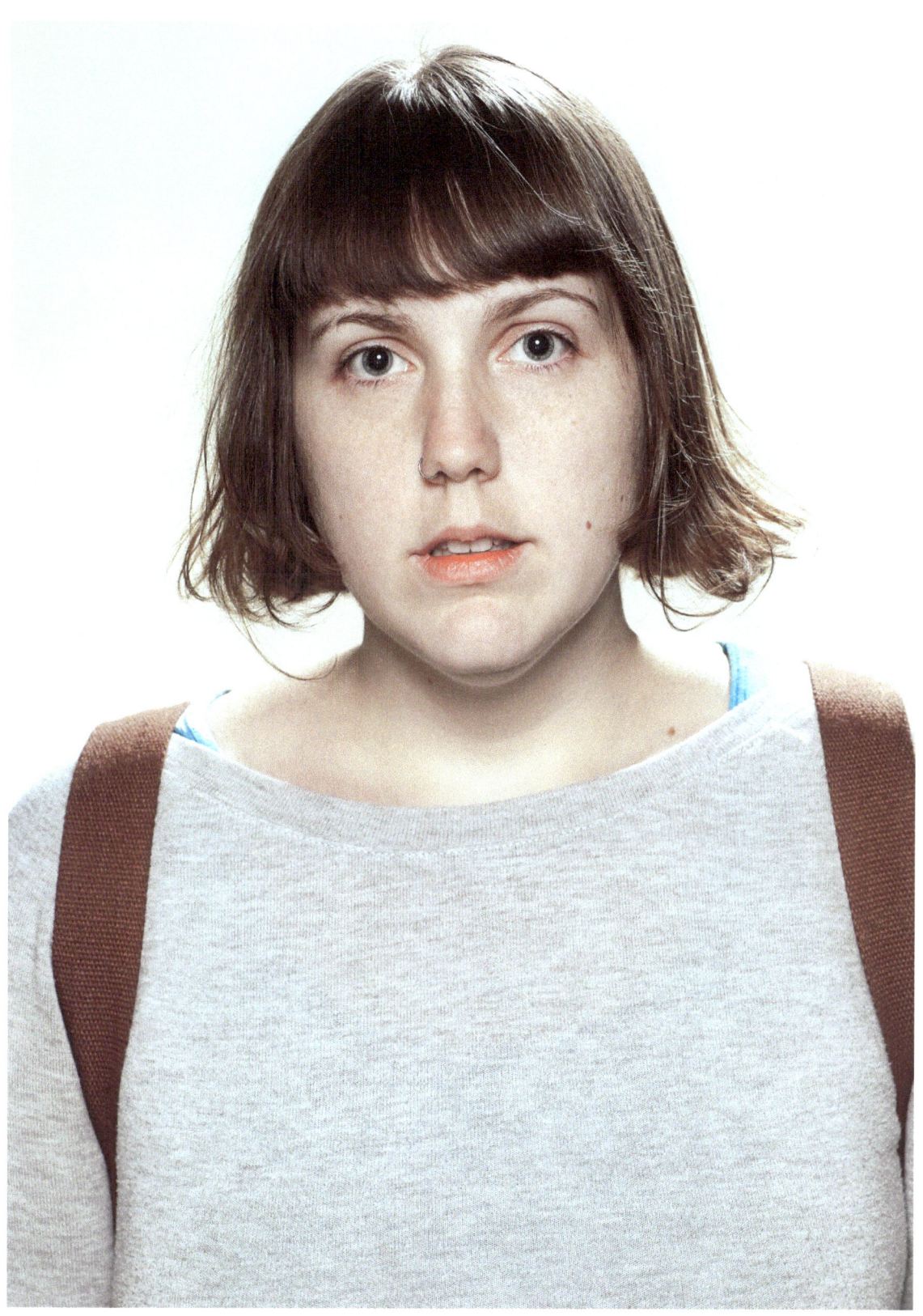

Courtney Severner

Heather Labus

About two years ago, I was scoping out Noir Ohio's vintage fashion blog and saw this dark haired beauty with thick straight bangs that framed her face perfectly. My envy for that edgy modern forehead concealing look grew to great proportions.

Now, although my forehead didn't compare to Tyra's (no insult intended, she rocks it), I was always a little self-conscious about the size. I figured it was time to snip some of my two foot locks off and hide away my forehead for the first time in 18 years. I went to my girlfriend's salon and committed to the cut.

I was so disappointed. They were poofy, thin, and reminiscent of a 1992 yearbook photo. I immediately went home, parted my hair strand by strand, studied the photo of the dark haired beauty and took my crappy craft scissors and cut.

I combed my bangs straight and inspected for any stray hairs and it was then that my smile quickly returned. They worked with every angle of my face and complimented my thick Greek eyebrows. I had never felt so confident and sexy and I have never let anyone else cut my bangs.

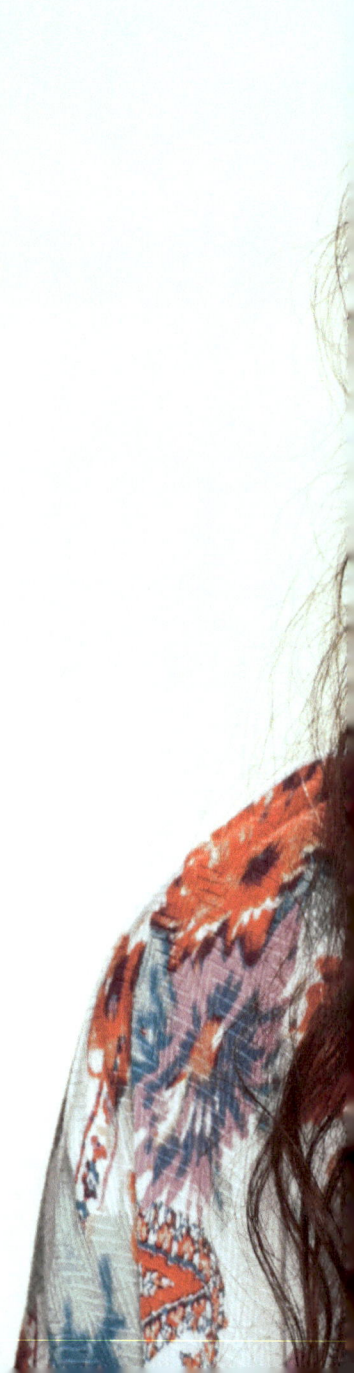

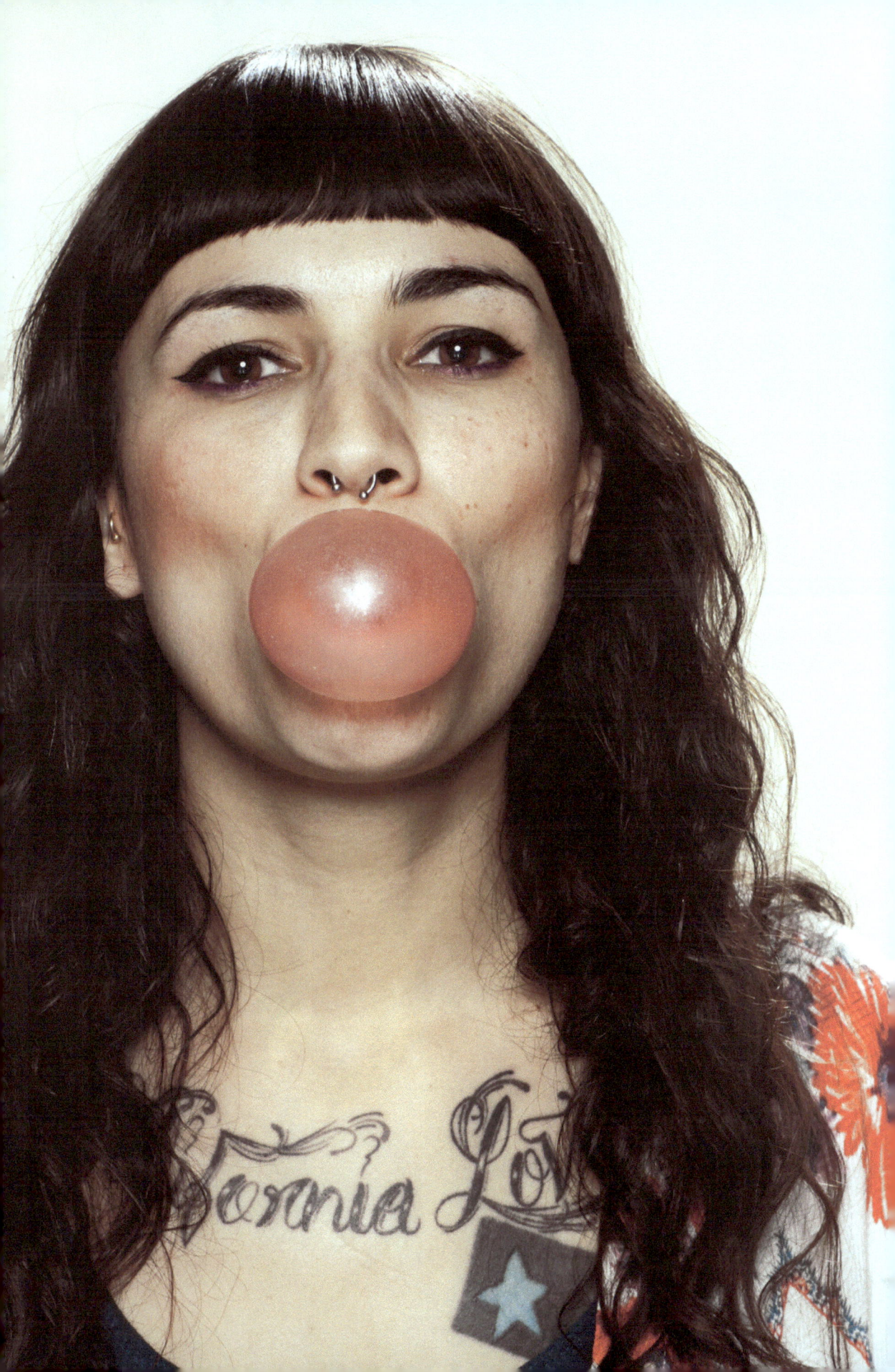

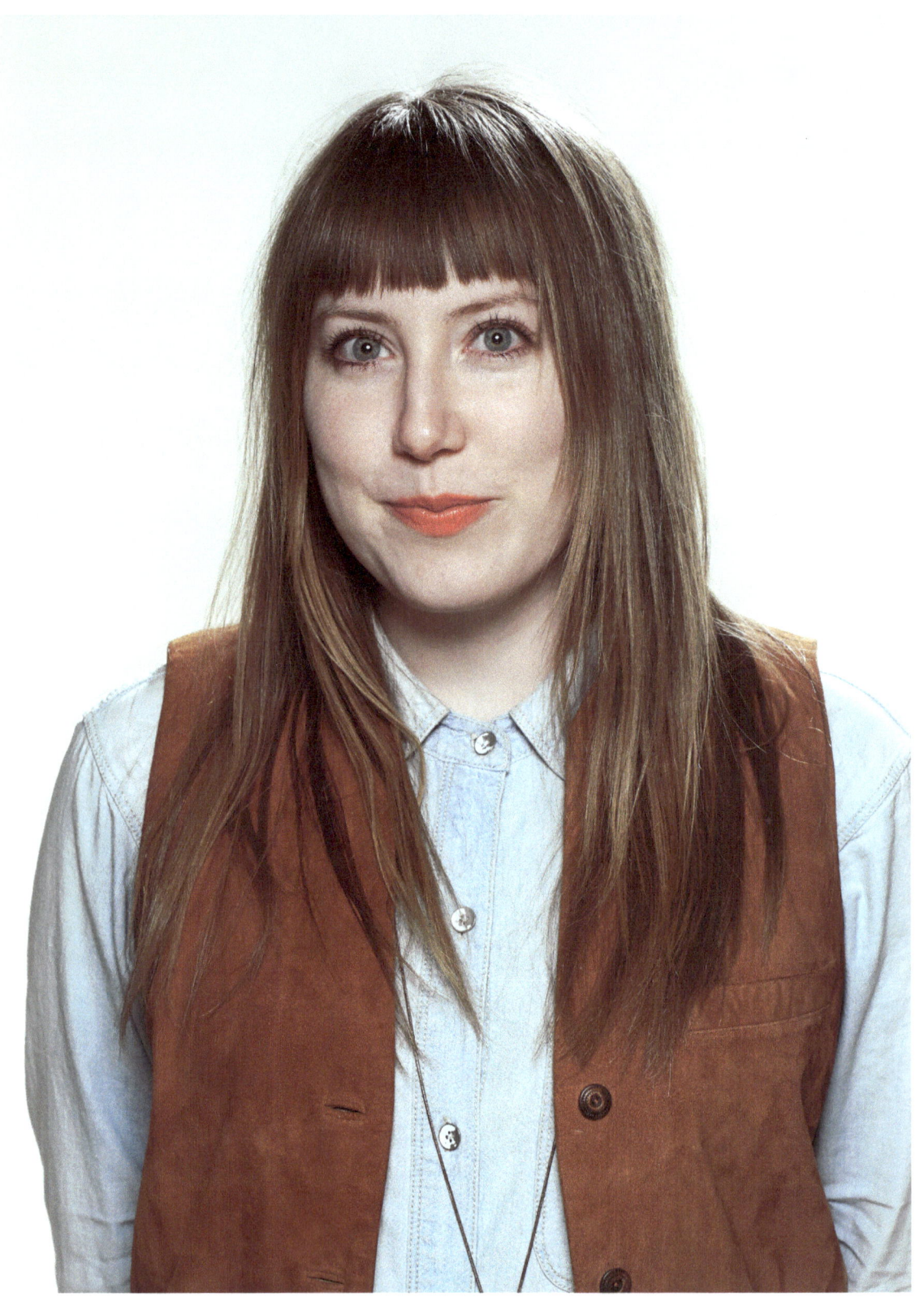

Alex Rose

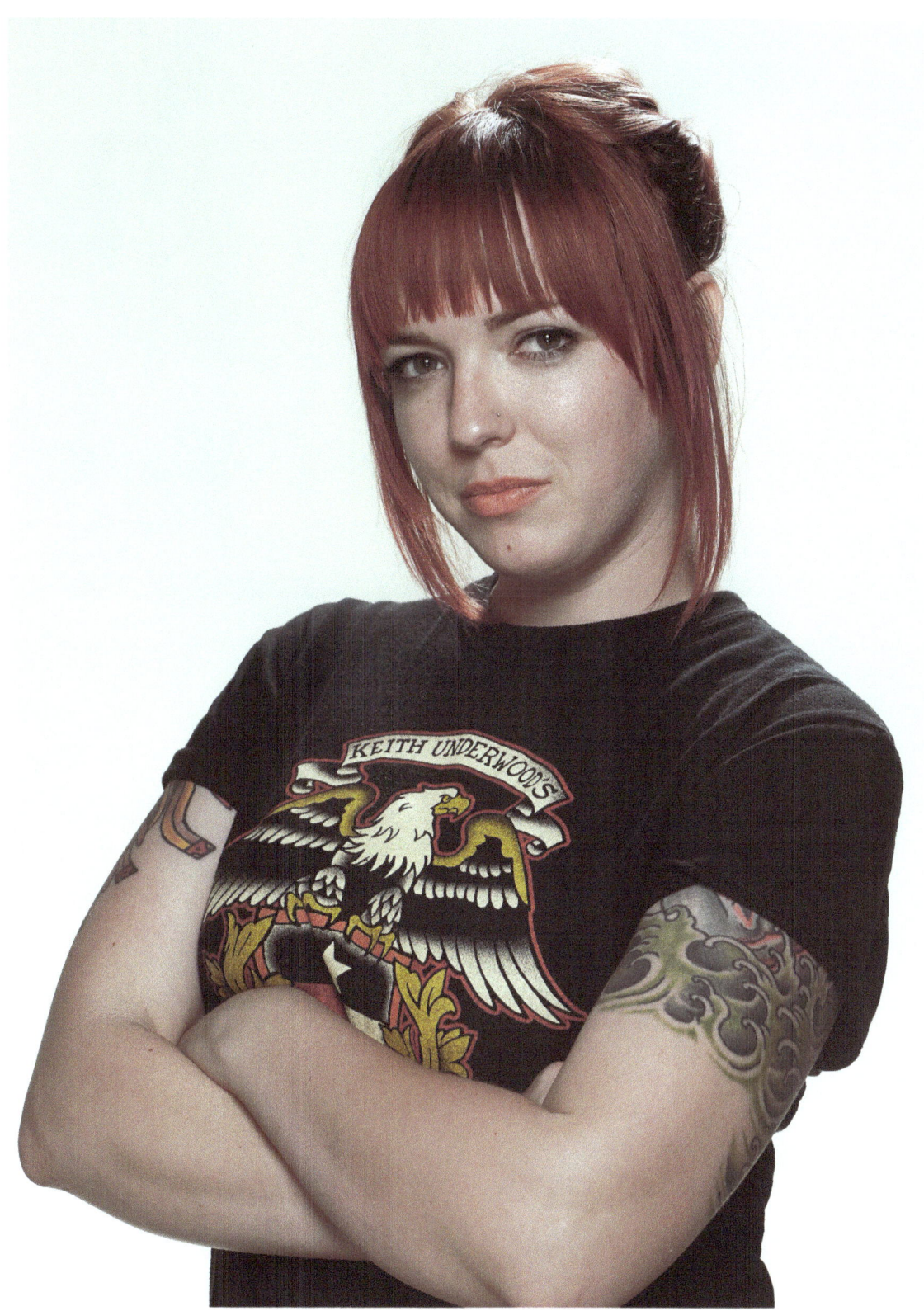

Stephanie Castleberry

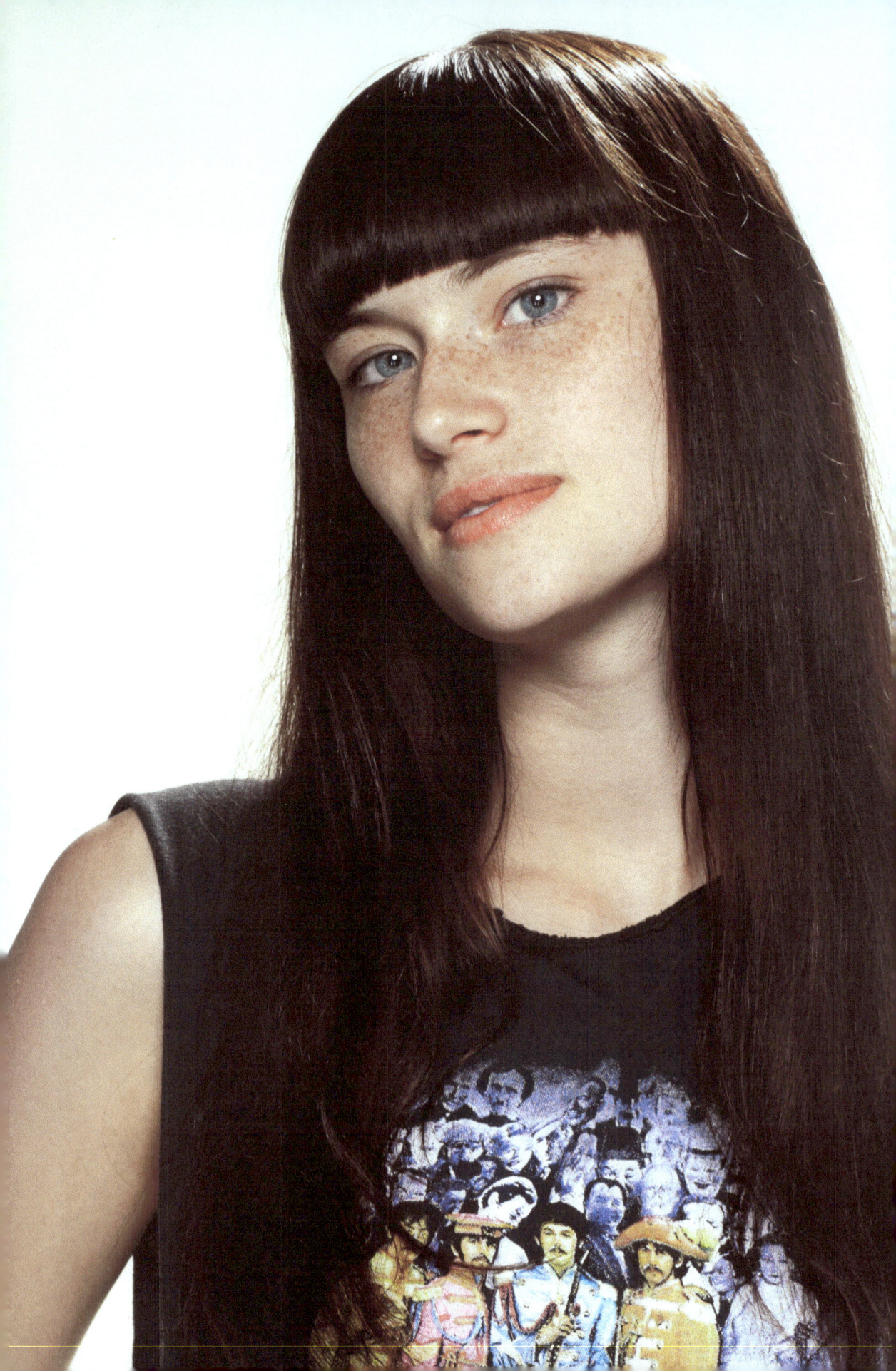

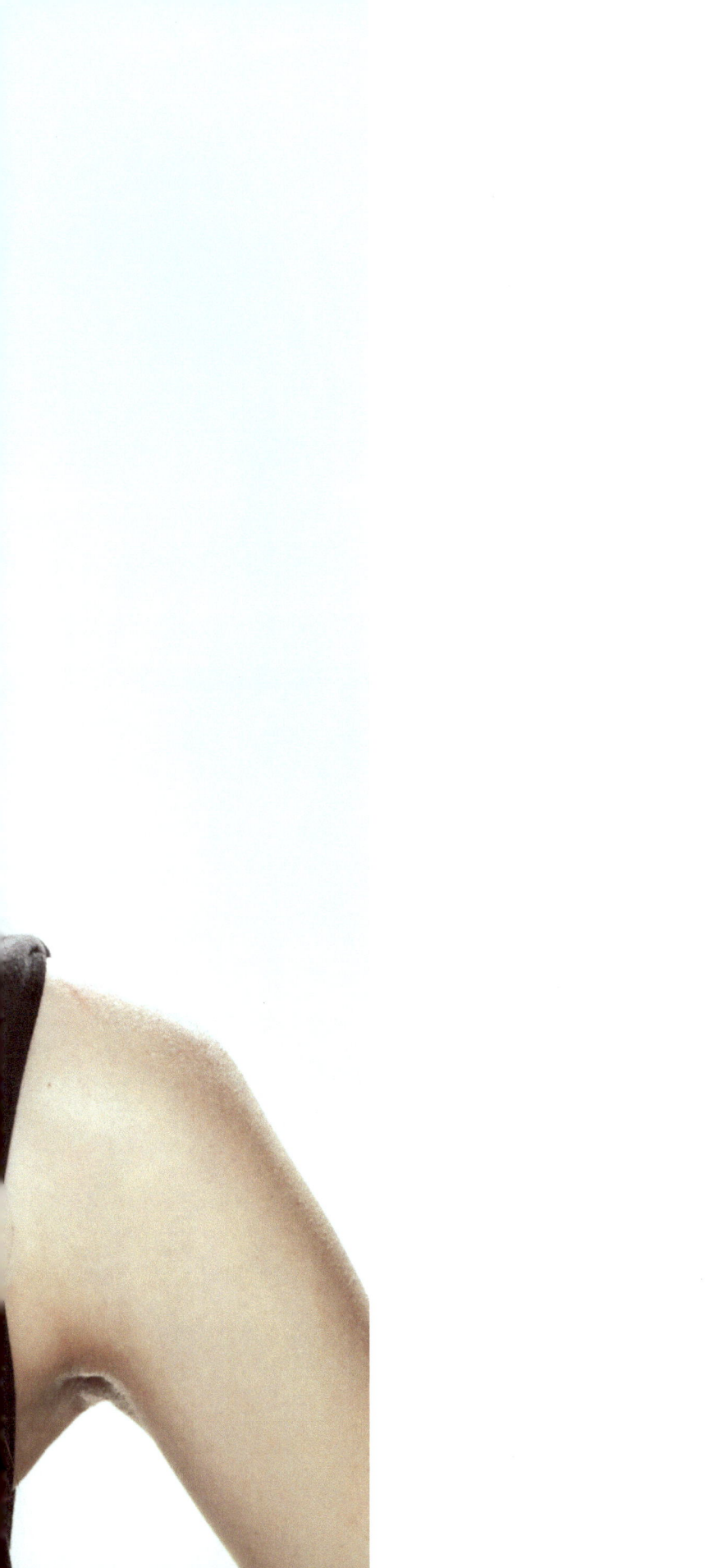

Julie Wier

I always go back to bangs.

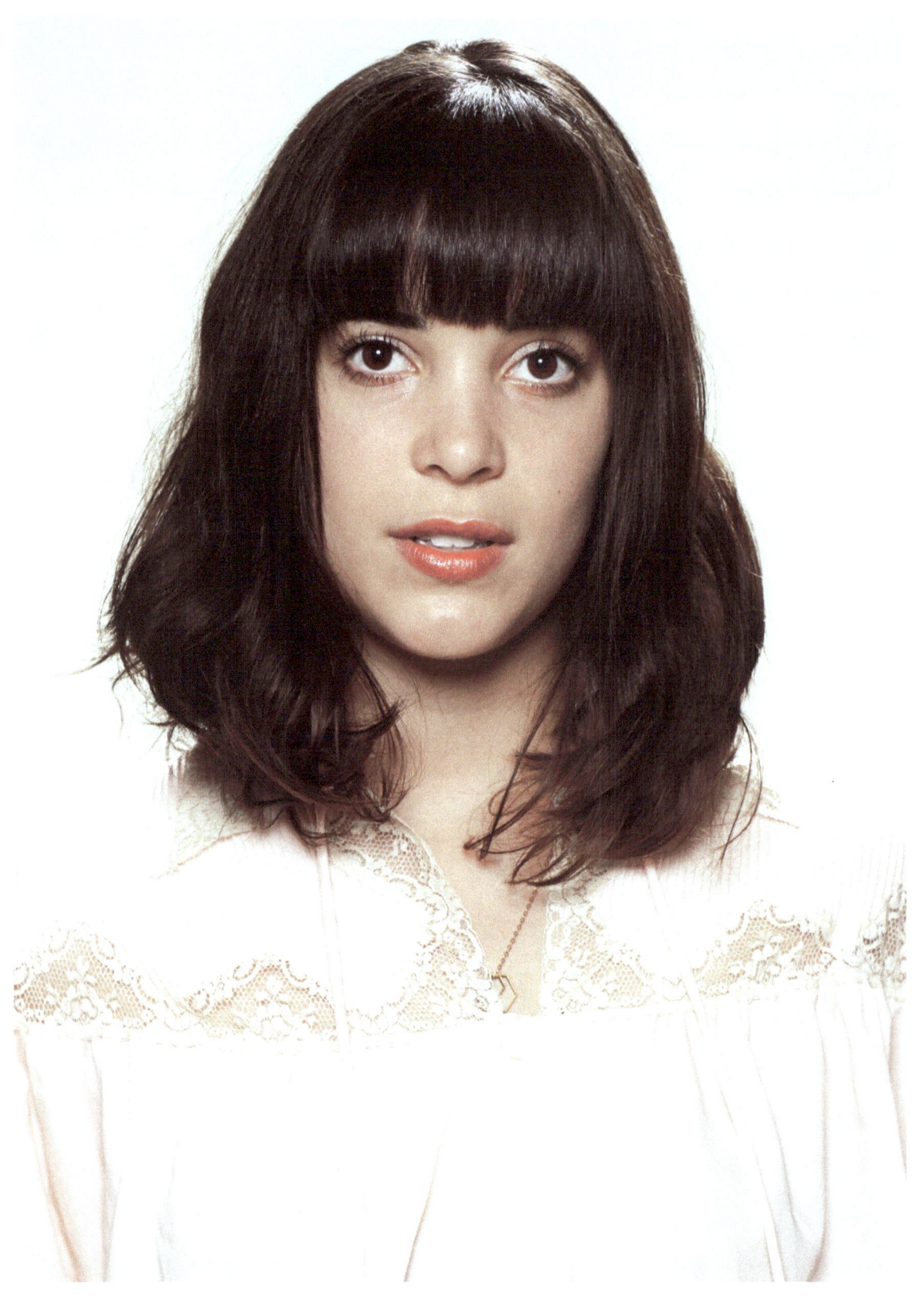

Luisa Carneiro

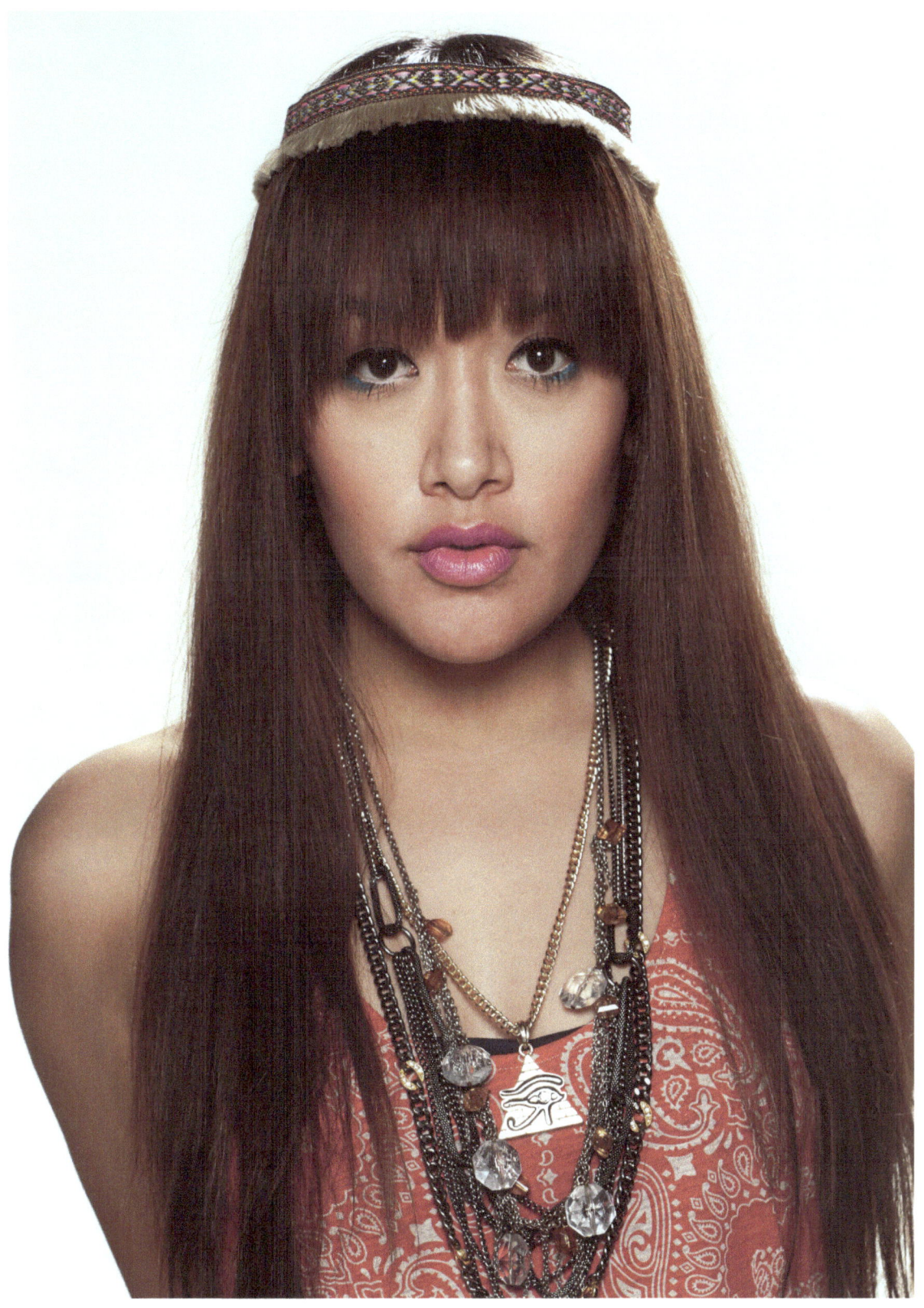

Frankie Estrada

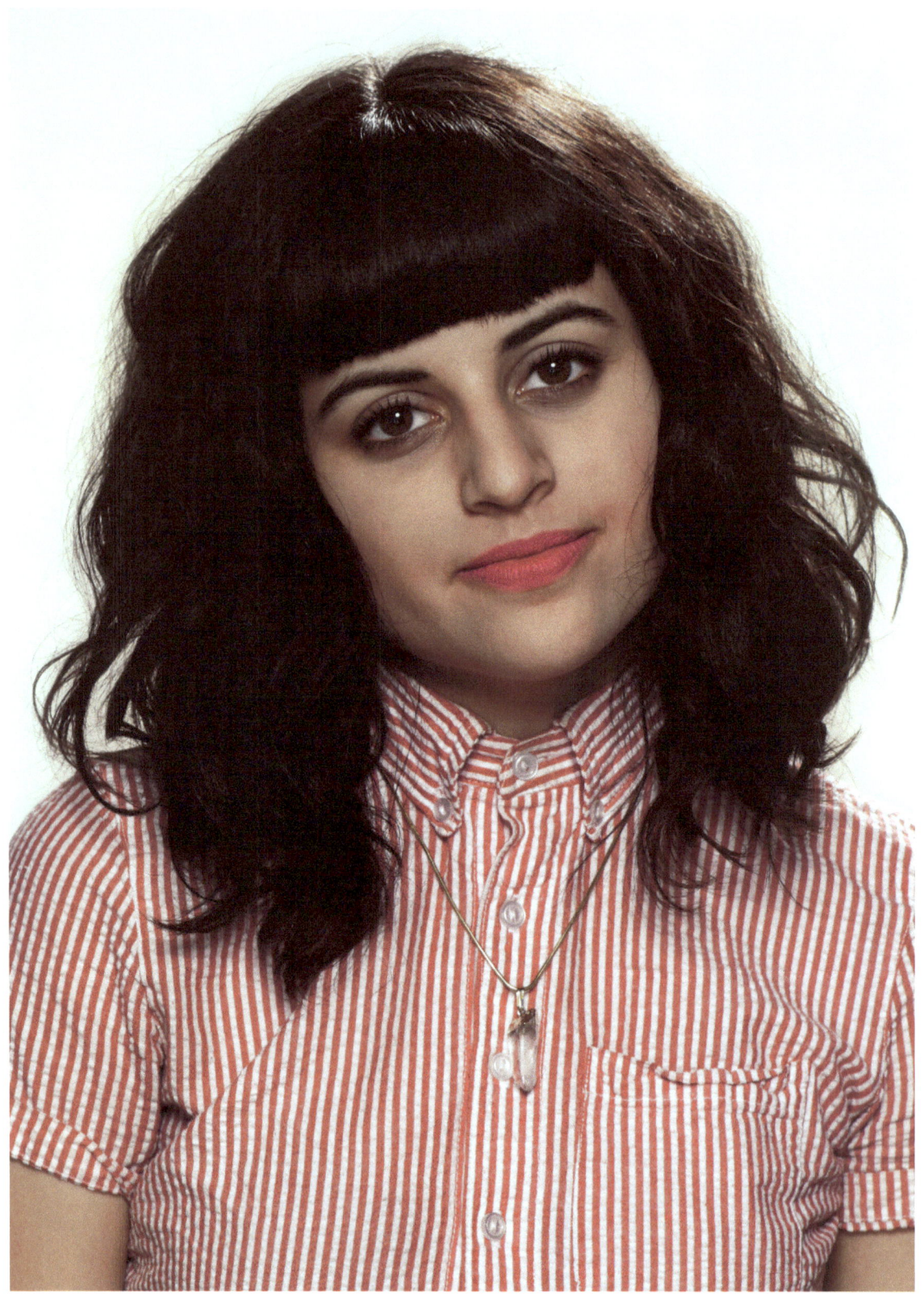

Brittany Keen

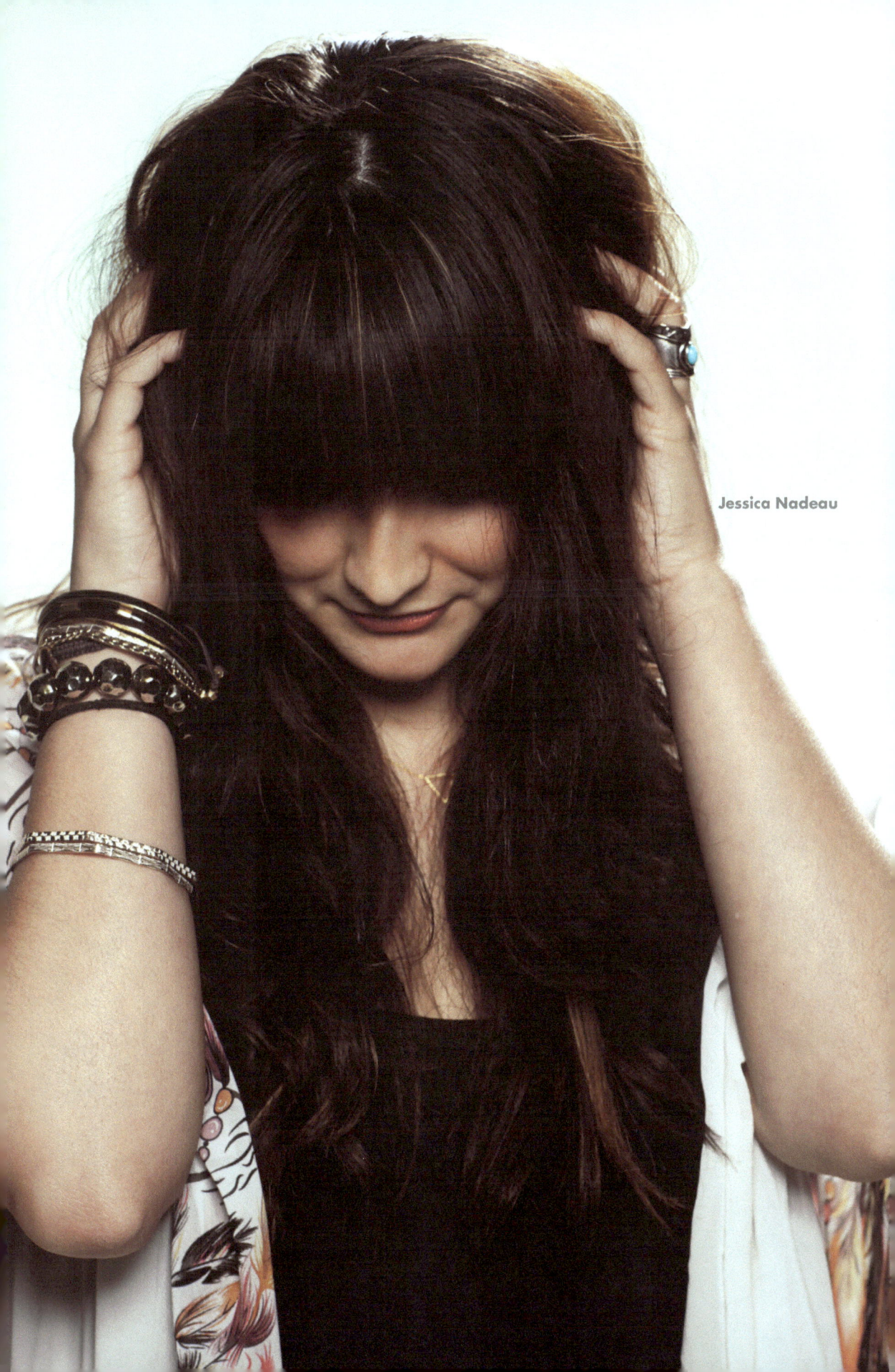

Jessica Nadeau

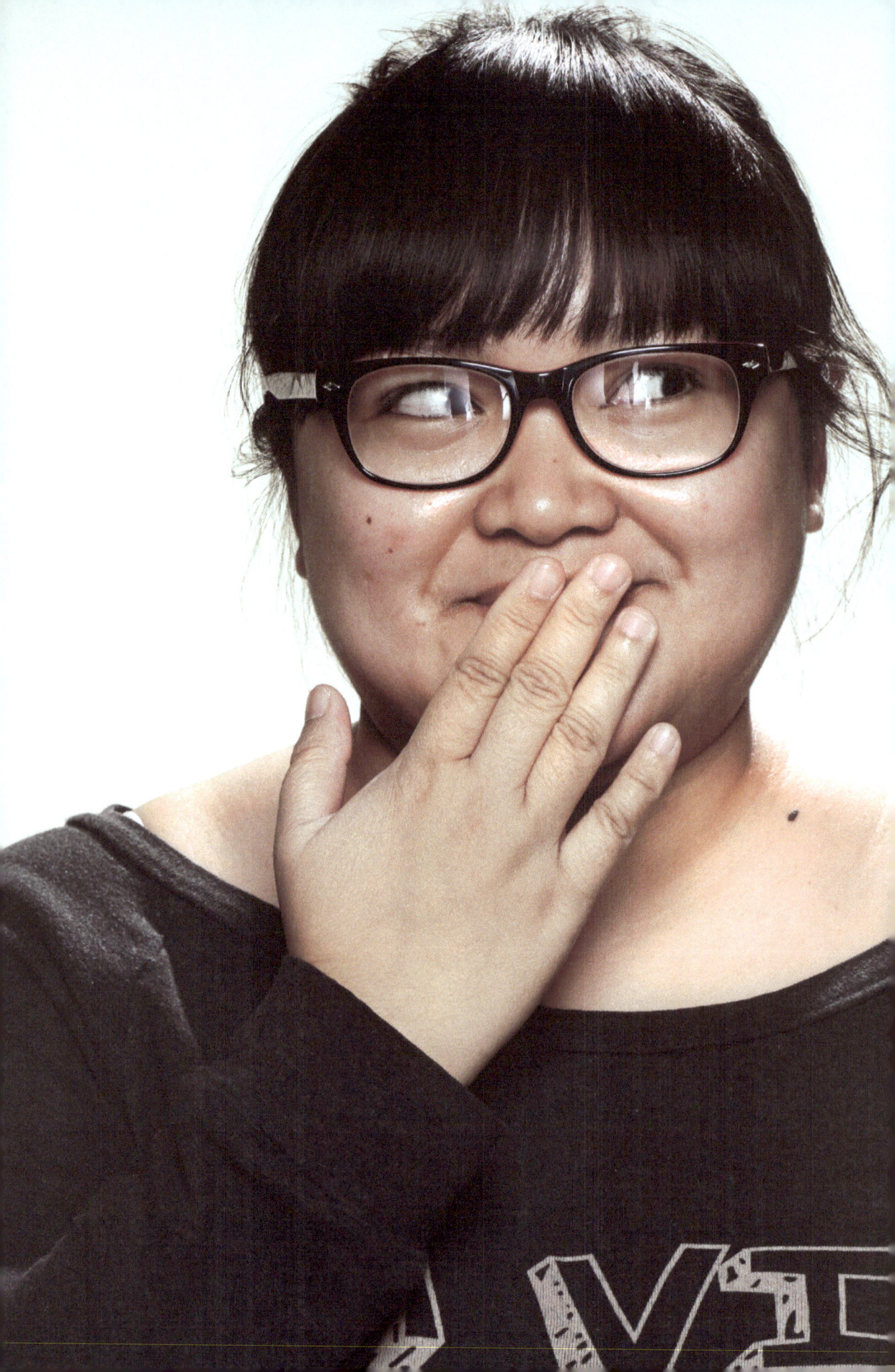

Esther Macas

I felt that blunt bangs would help me feel confident and fearless as I prepared to get into the workforce.

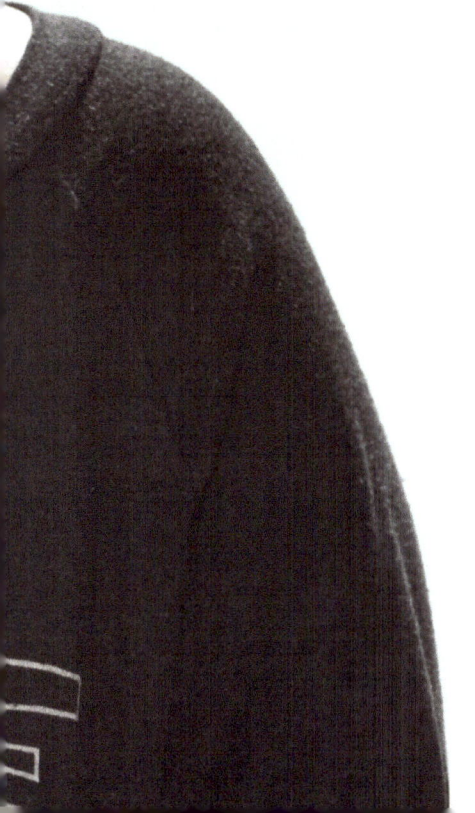

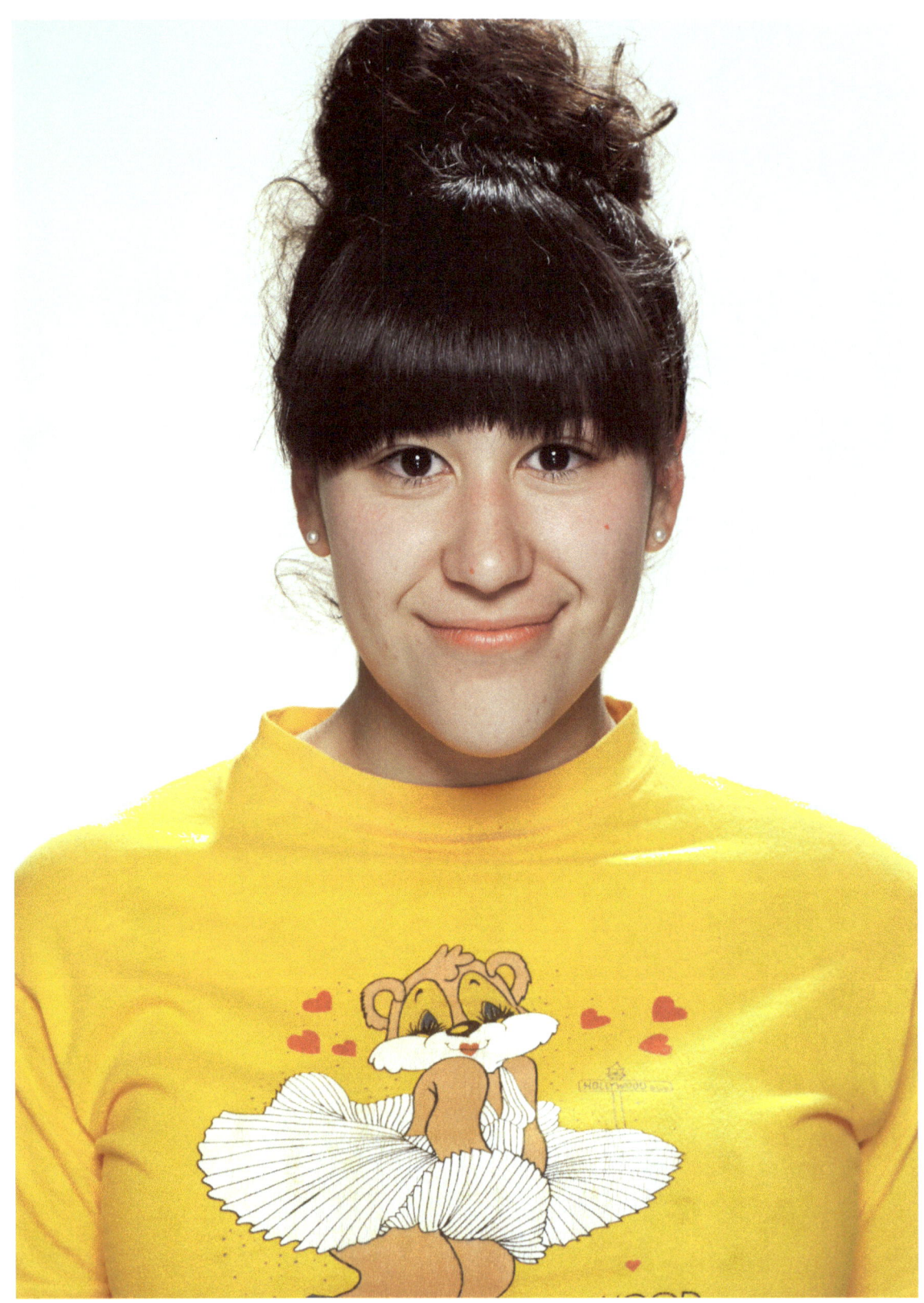

Jocelyn Quintanilla

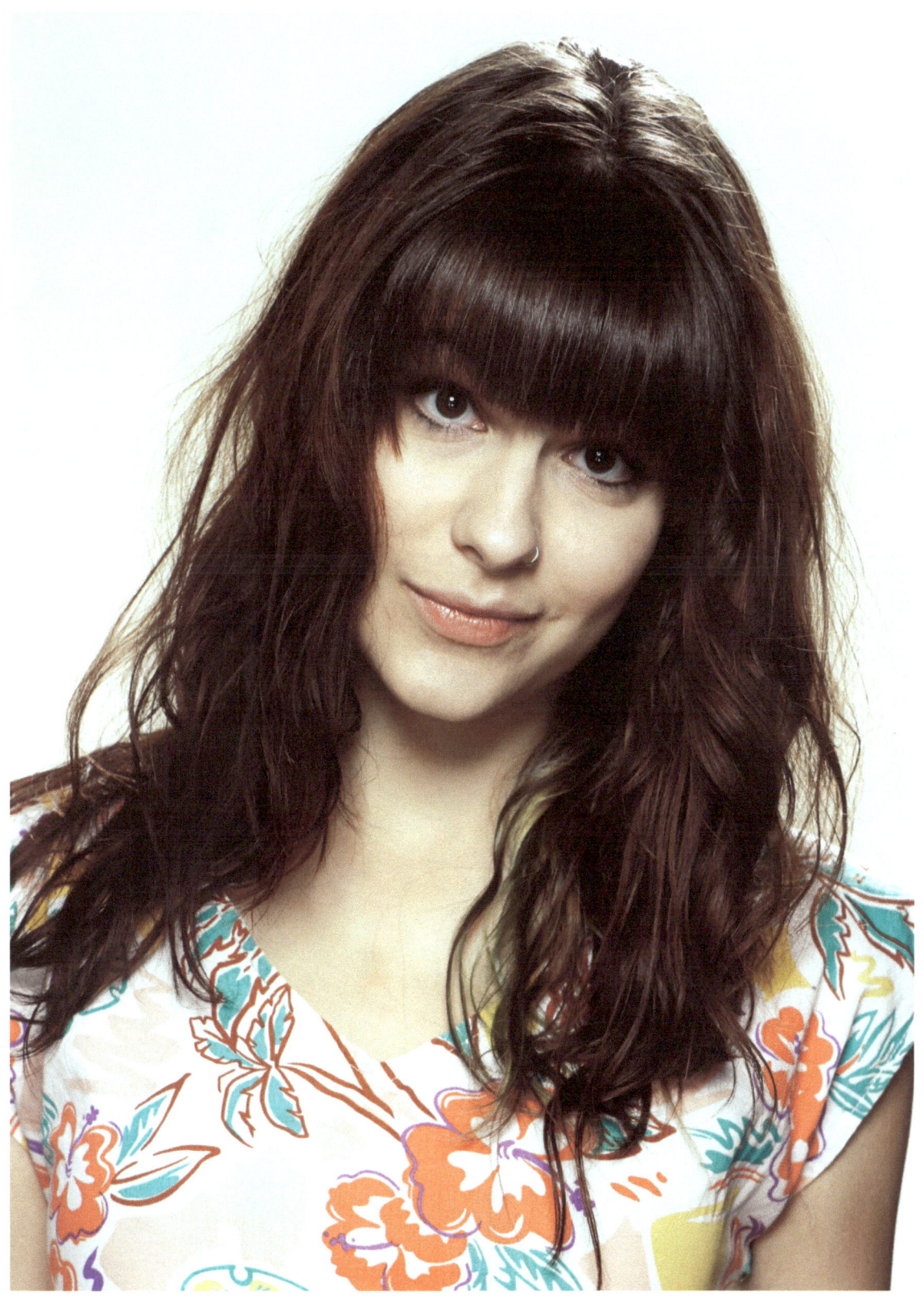

Bryanna Stone

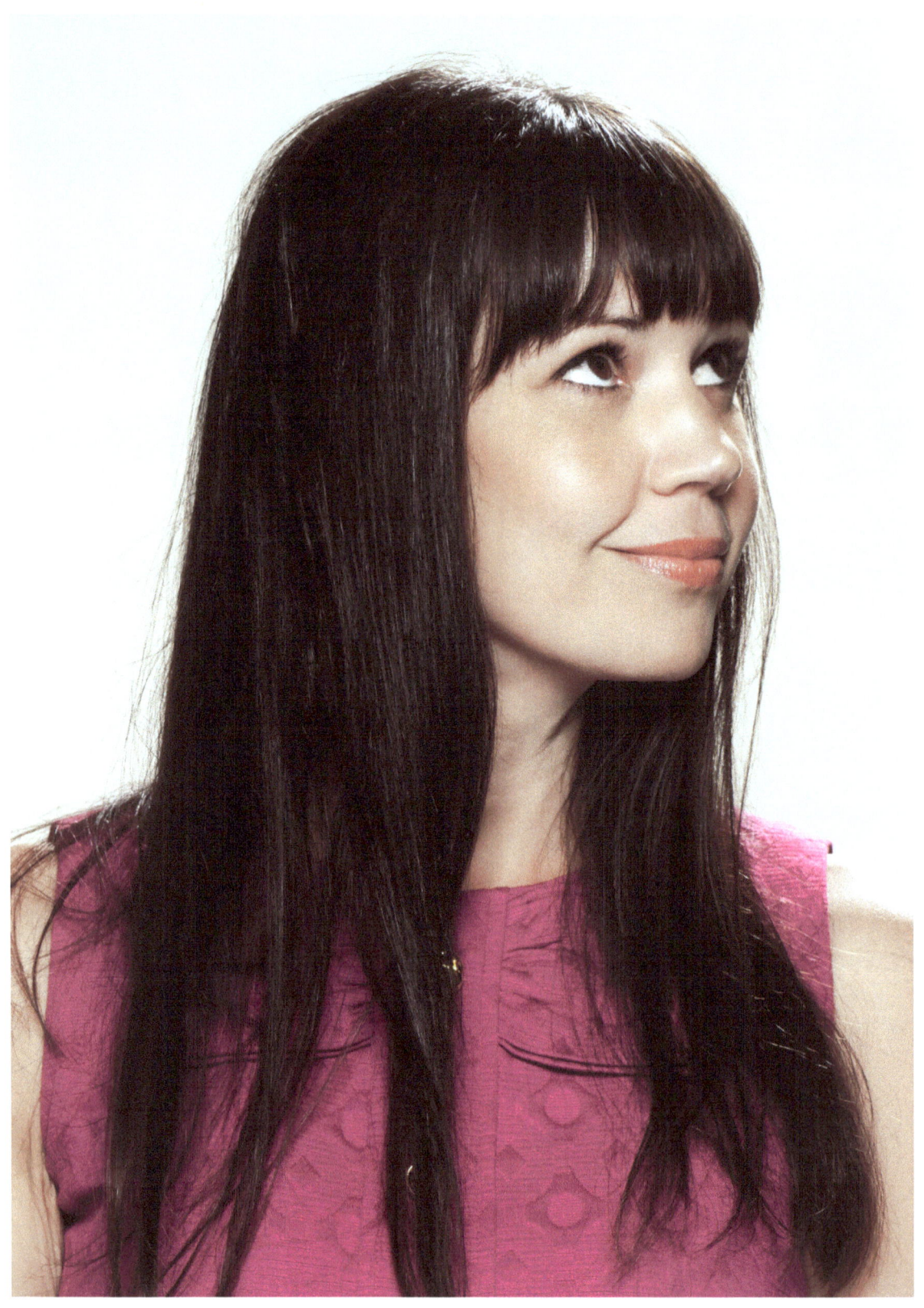

Rachael Jones

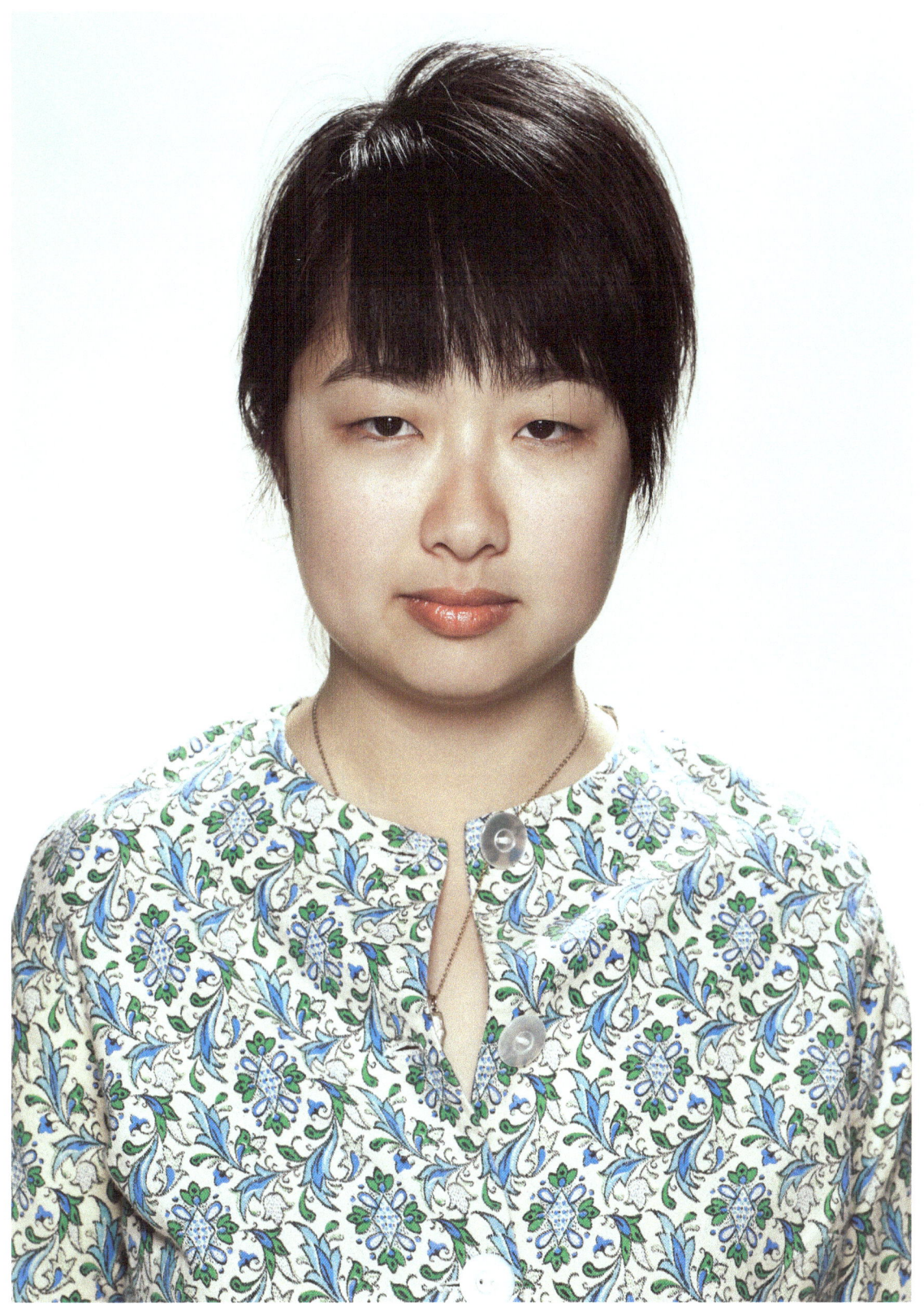

Wenjing Zhang

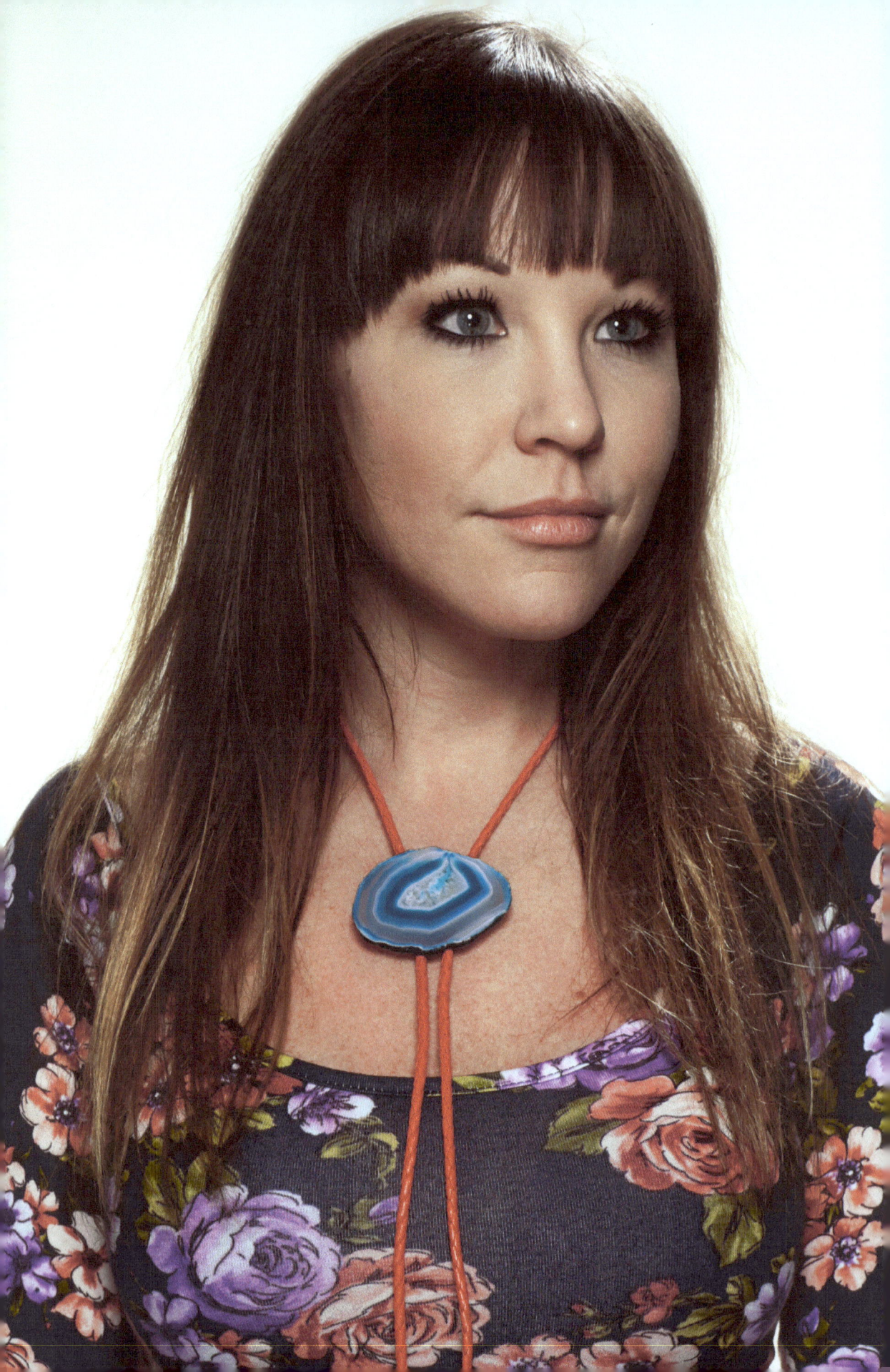

Lori Salmon

Curiosity banged me.

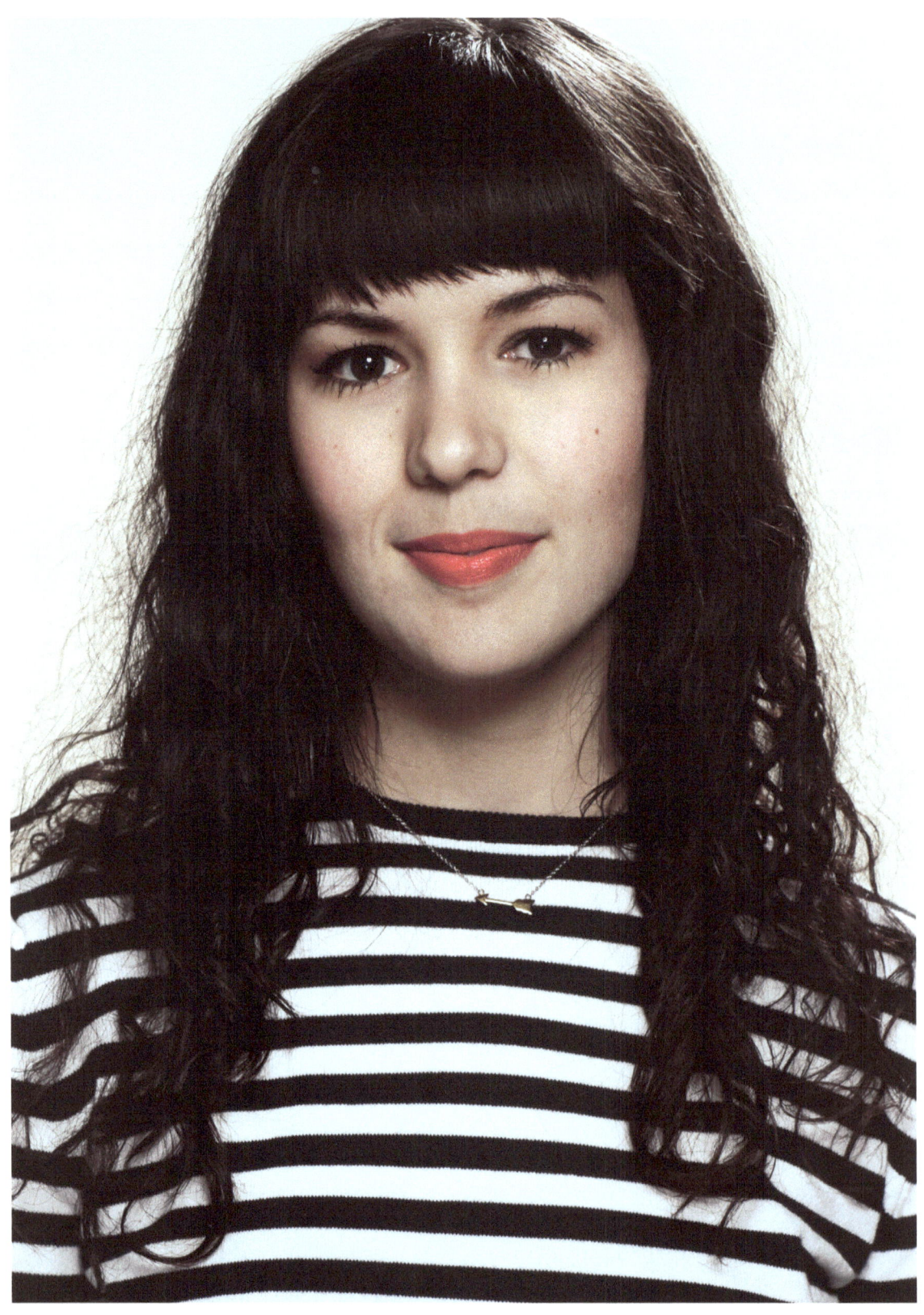

Natalie Collins

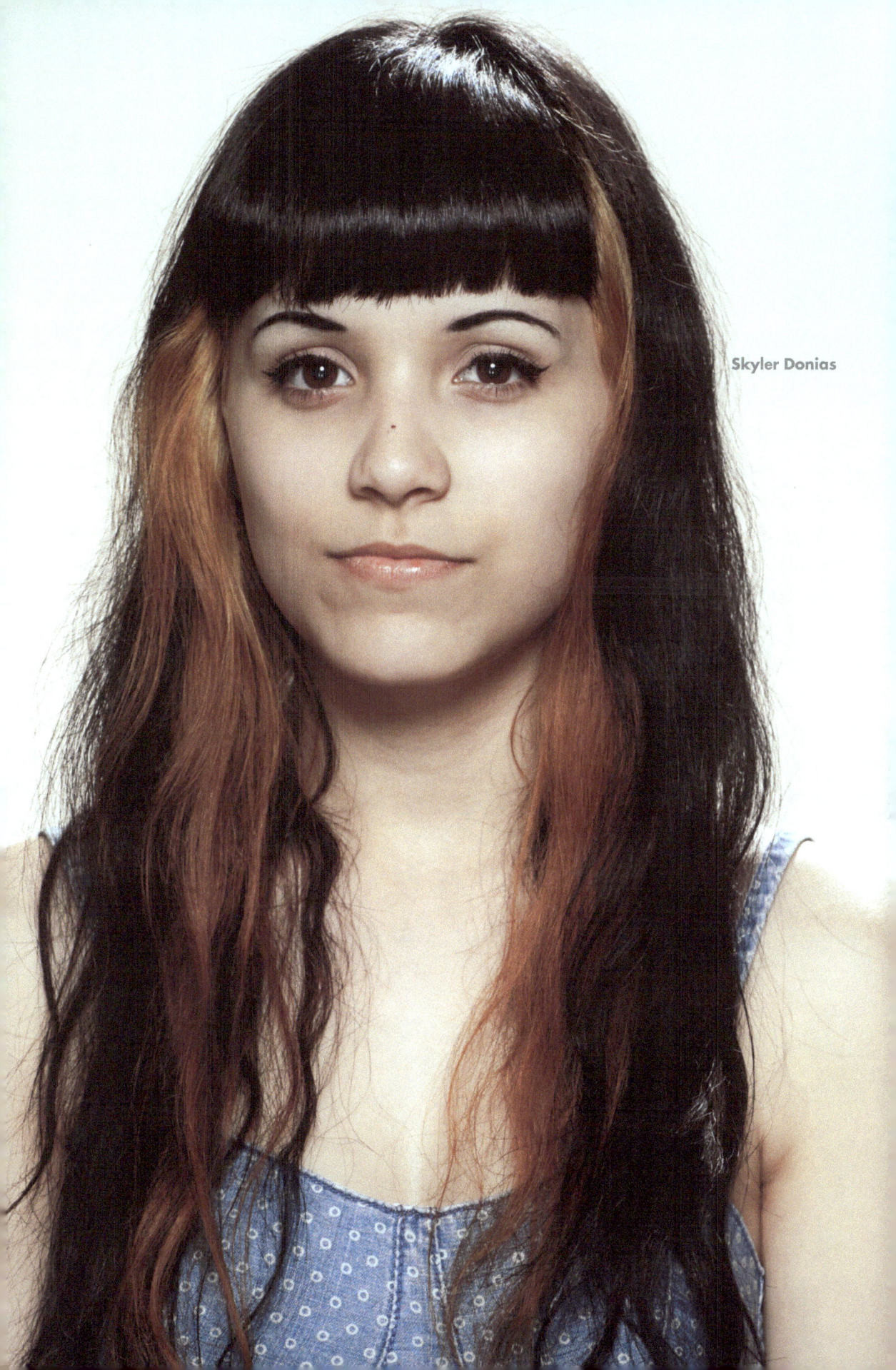

Skyler Donias

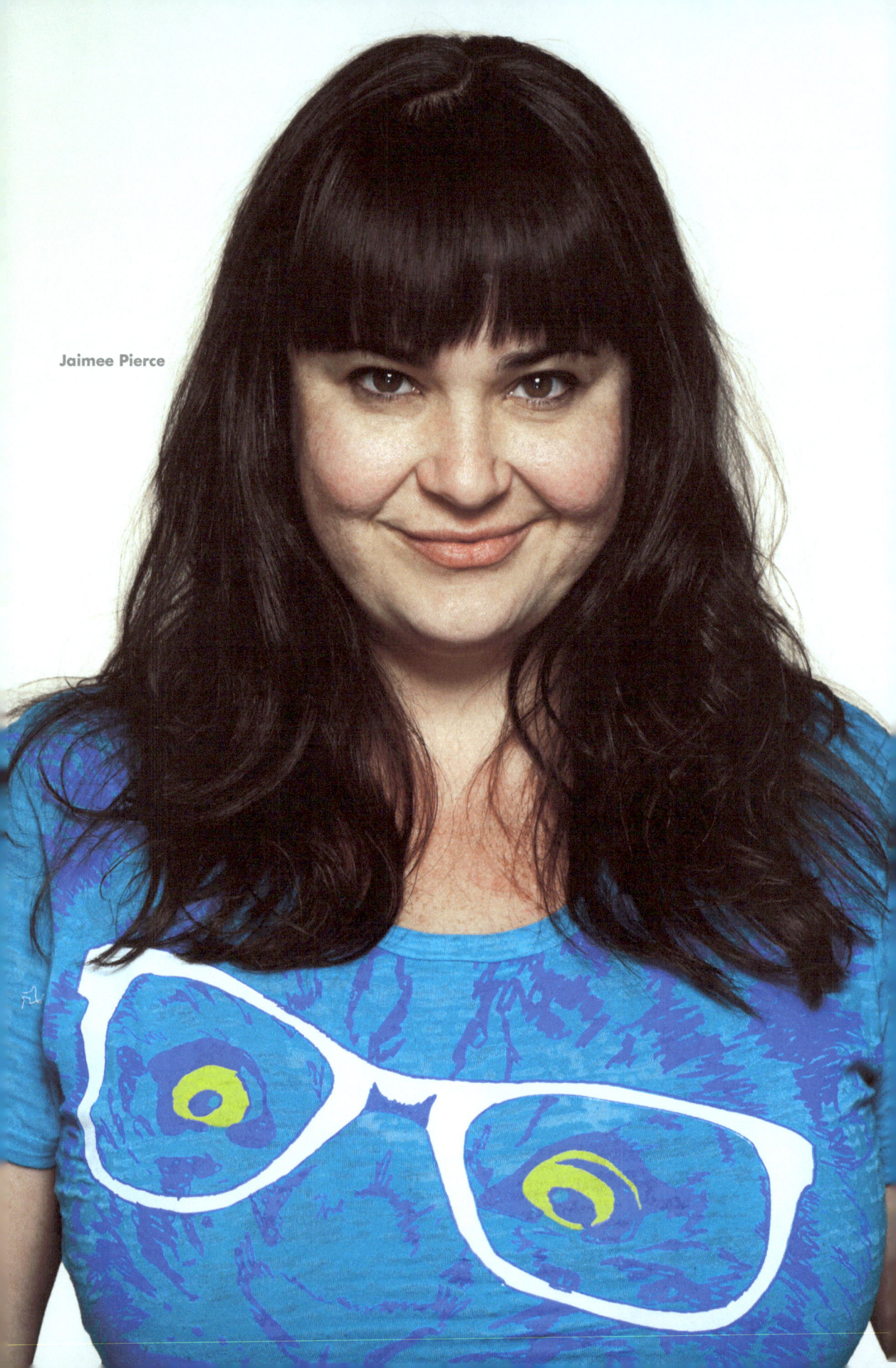

Jaimee Pierce

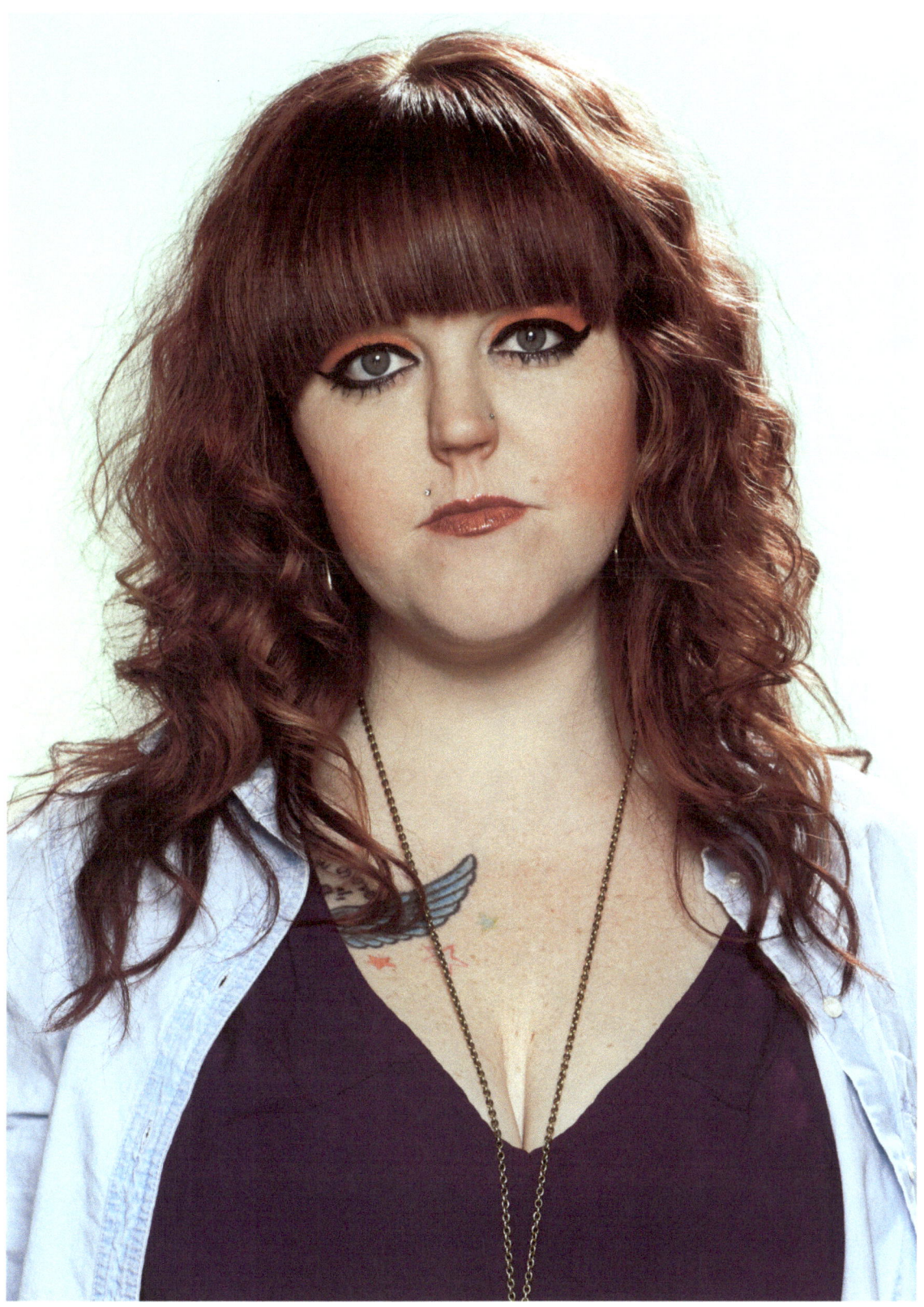

Kristen Catz

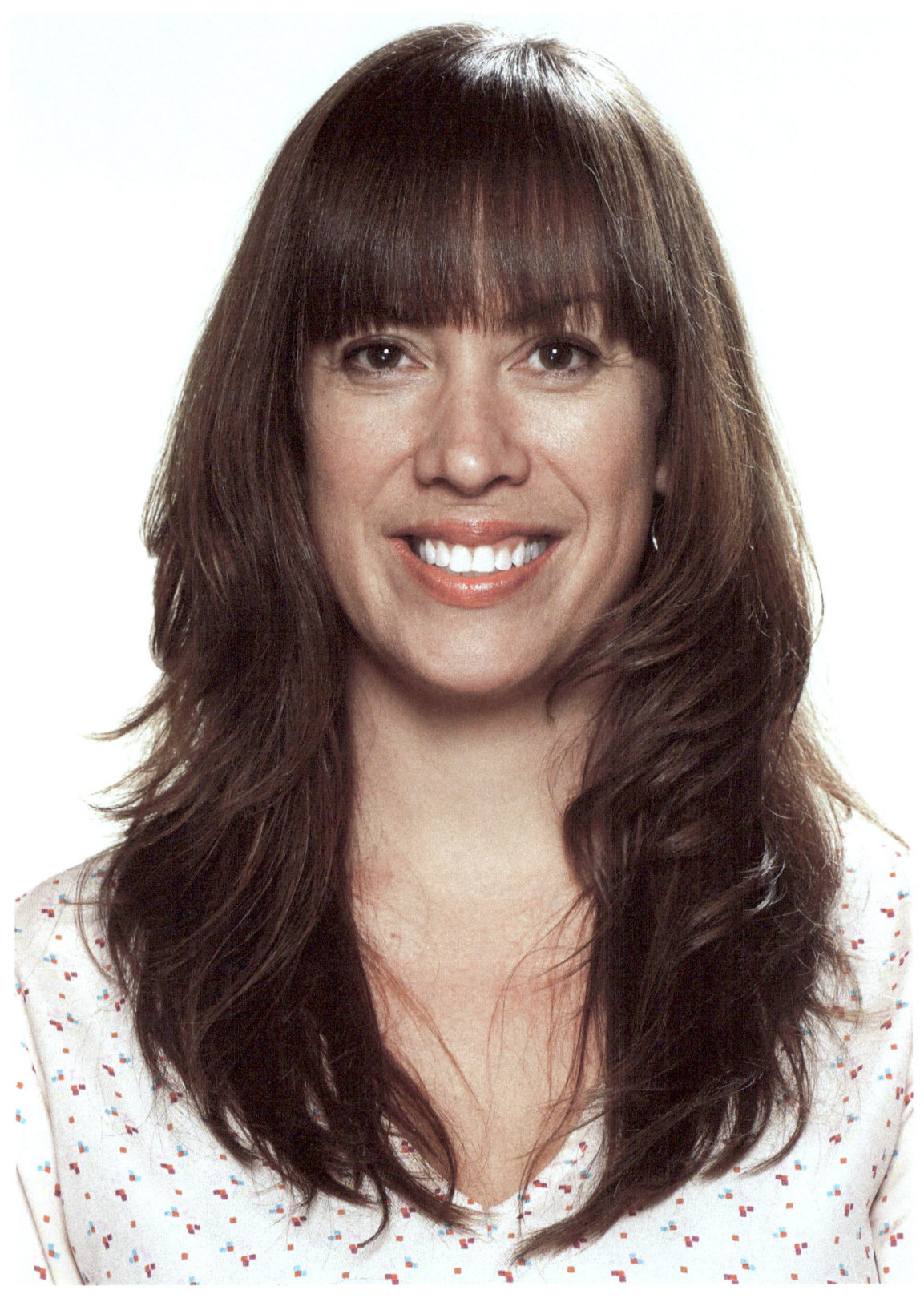

Tara Powell

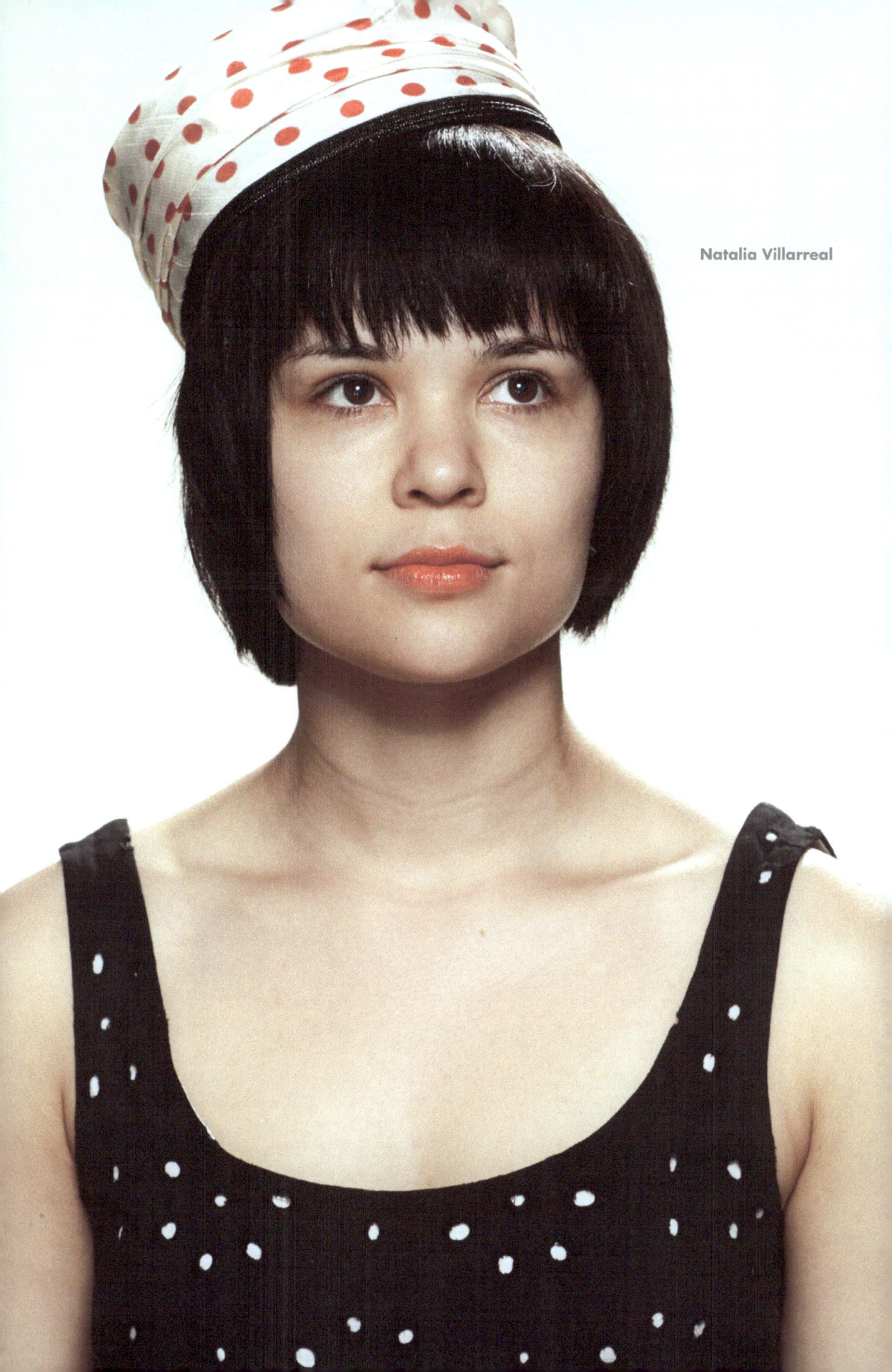

Natalia Villarreal

Whitney Coulter

There was only a short period of my
life when I didn't have some form of
bangs. It was middle school and we'll
call them the dark ages – the time when I
was experimenting with my identity and
therefore was incredibly awkward.

Bangs have been with me since I can
remember swooshing my baby bangs
around in the pool, pretending to be Ariel
the Little Mermaid. My hair stylist (I call
her the brains behind my bangs) won't let
me be without them these days because
she knows who I am and what I need,
which not surprisingly is the exact same
haircut I had when I was four.

I've even joked that if someone wrote
an autobiography about me, it would be
called 'Bangs, Bands, and Beer'. Besides,
bangs compliment big hair and I like that.

The great Dolly Parton (bless her) was
rumored to say that the higher the hair,
the closer to heaven and my grandmama
always told me that the Bible said a
woman's hair was her glory. I figure if I'm
somewhere in between that, I'm on the
right track!

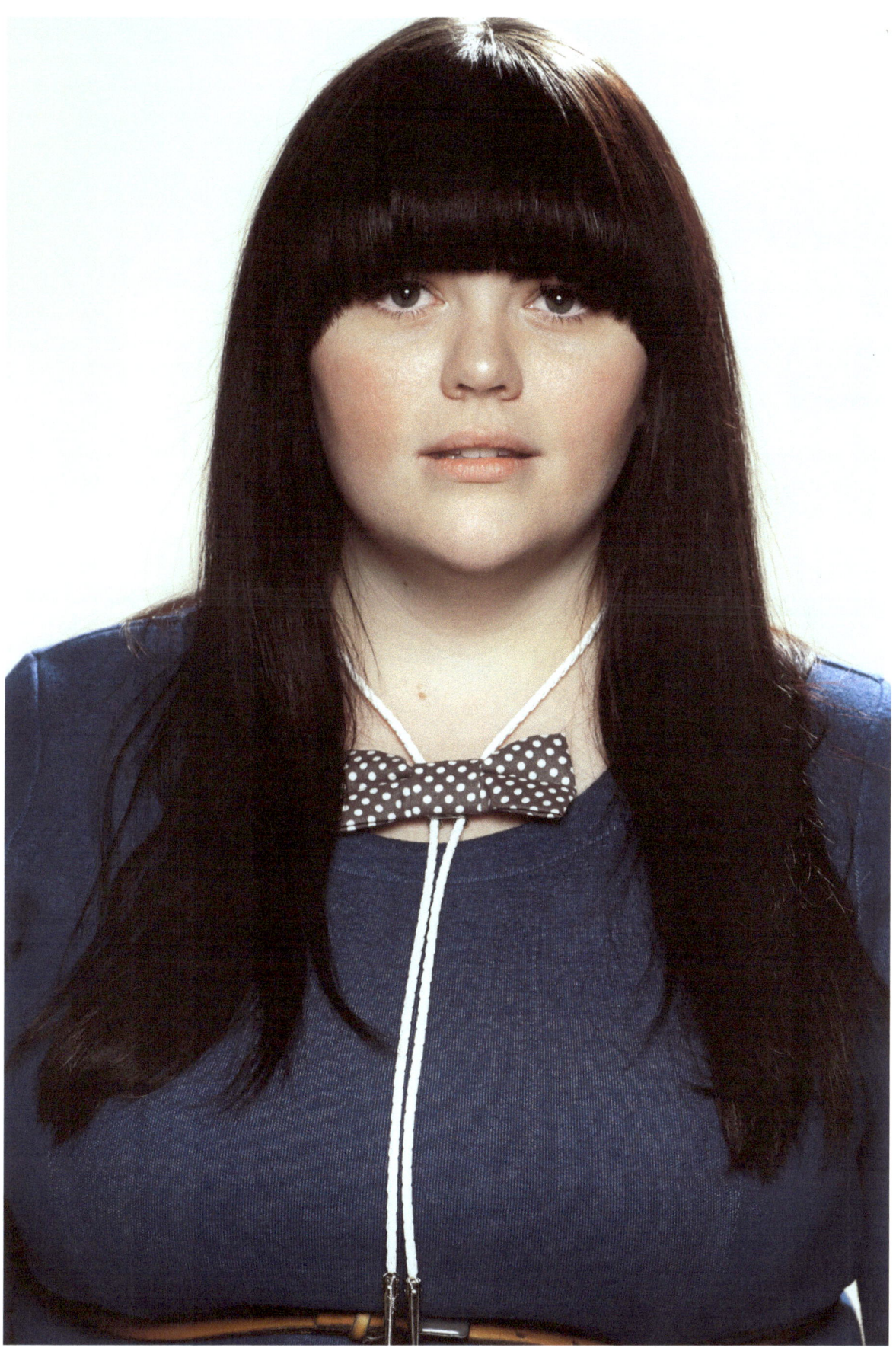

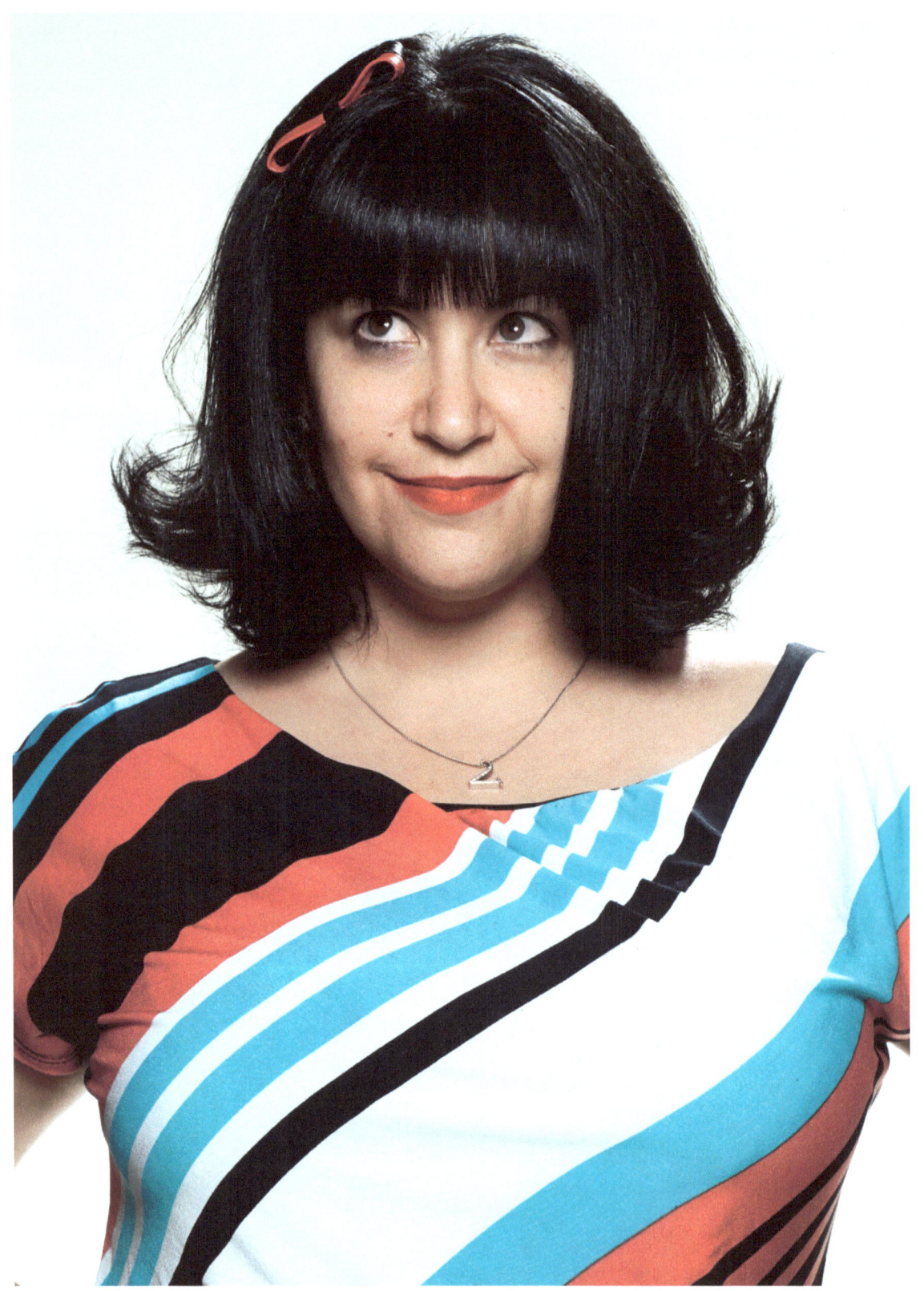

Valerie Aiello

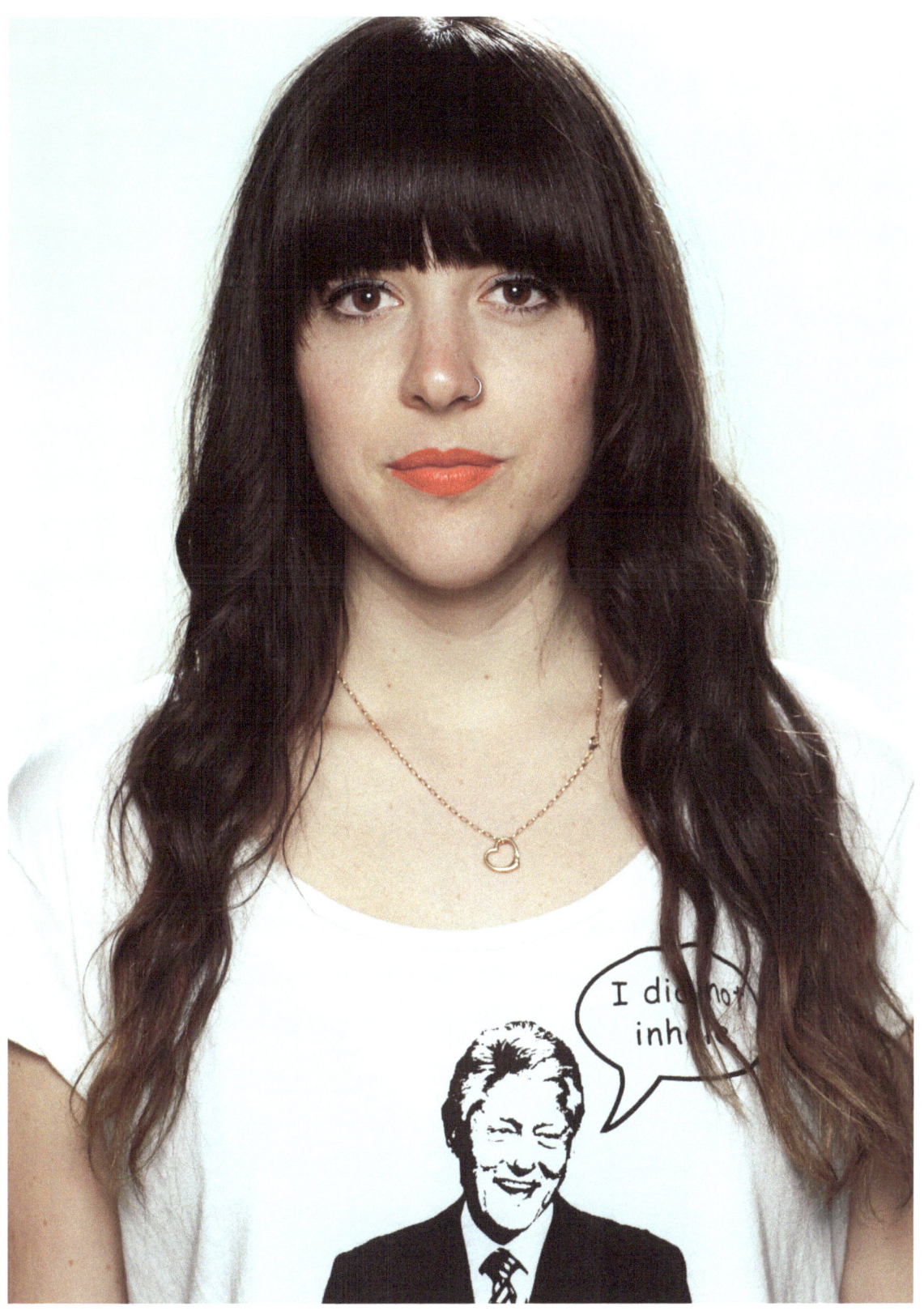

Cristina Fisher

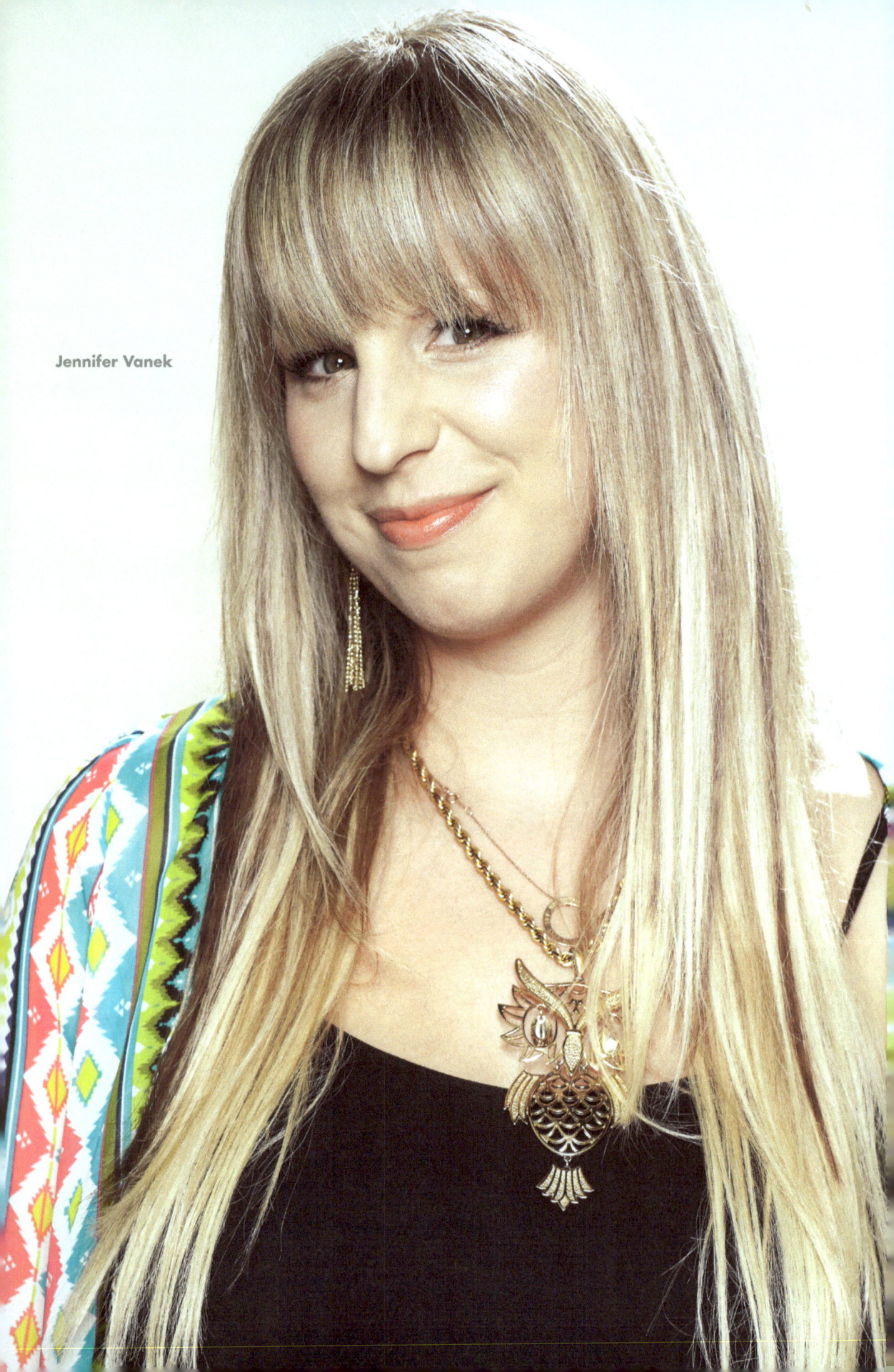

Jennifer Vanek

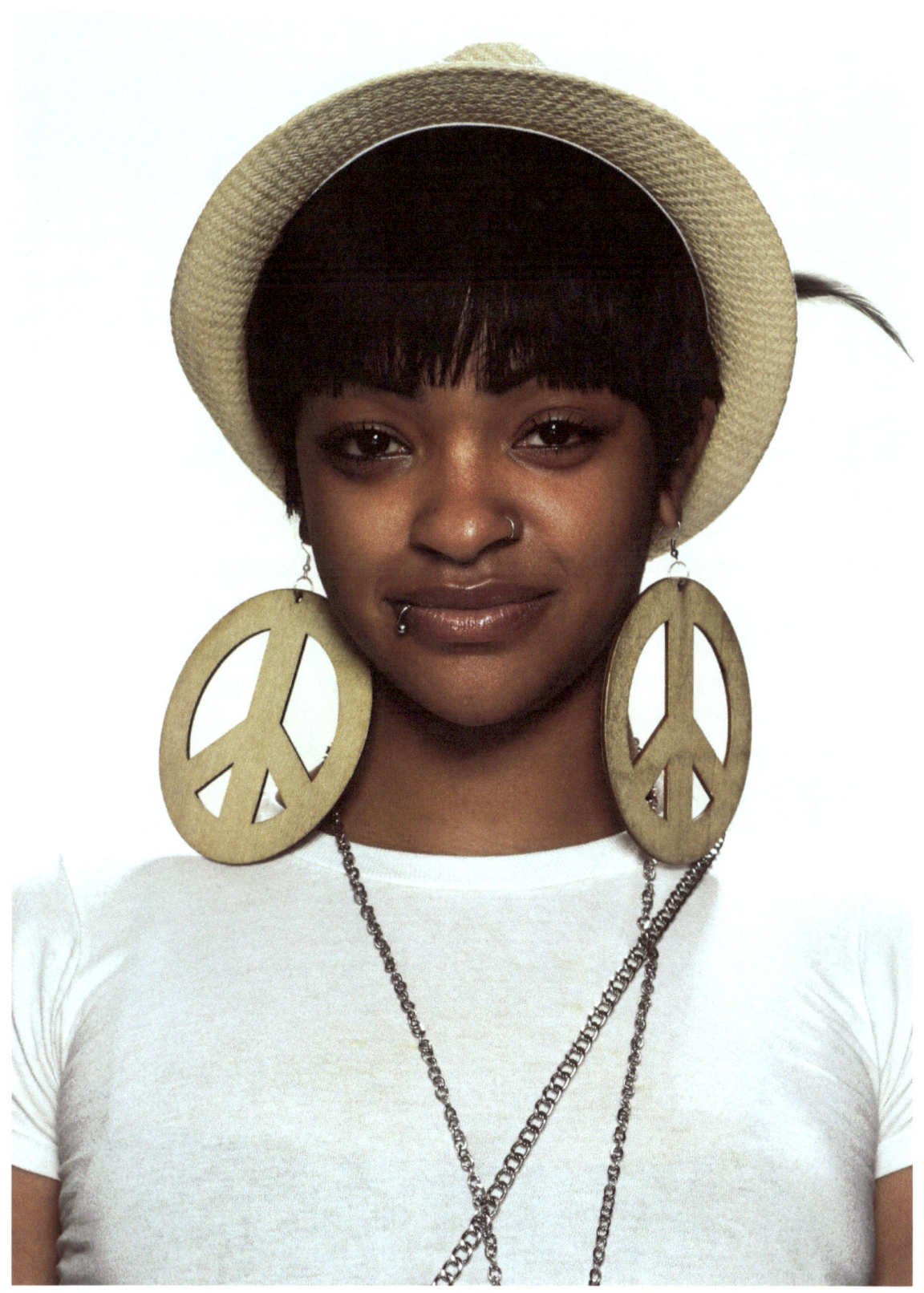

Alicia Lowery

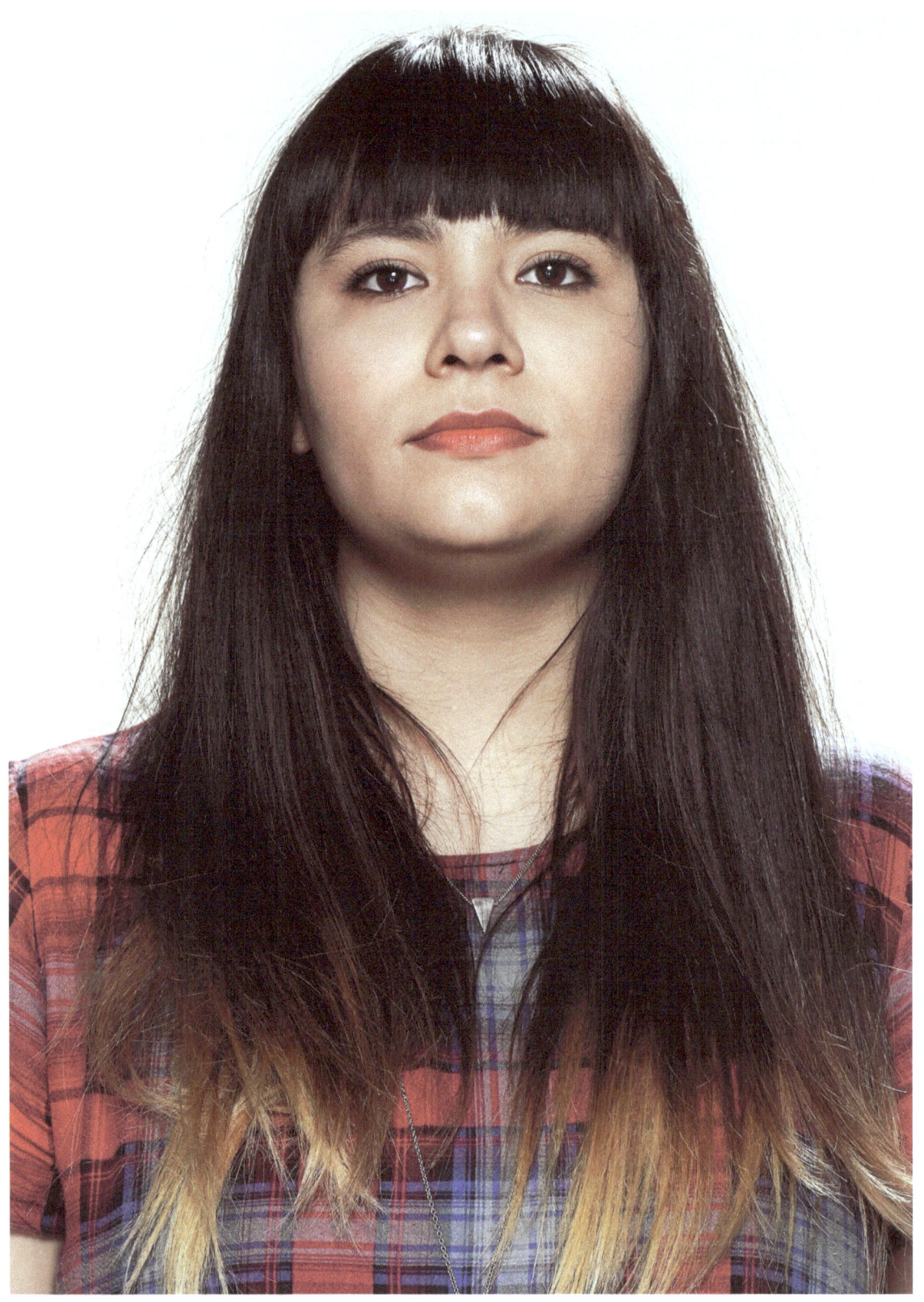

Kirsten Mireles

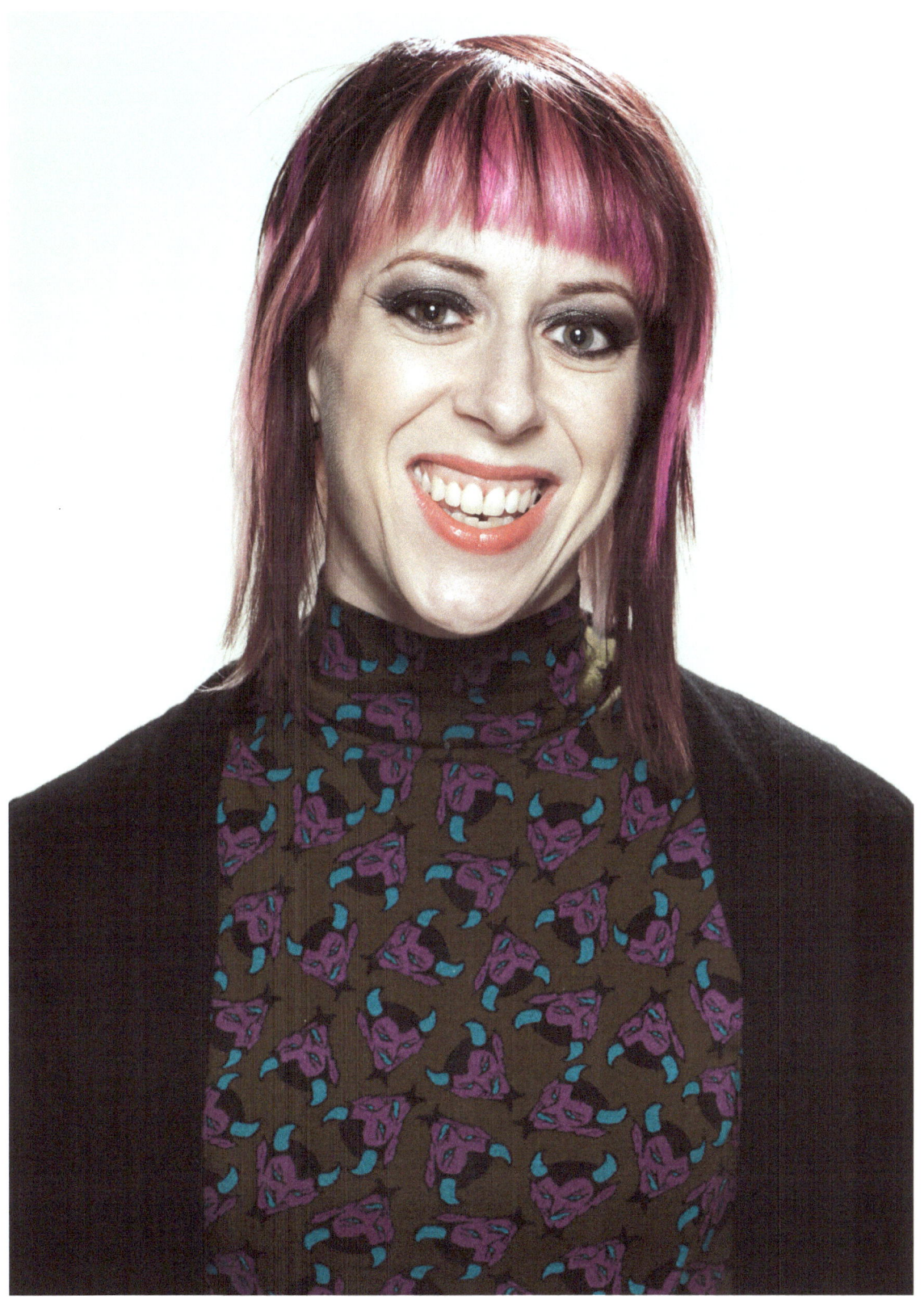

Nikki Donlan

Brittany Martin

I walked into a new hair salon having
decided on getting bangs. When
I told the stylist what I wanted, he
insisted my hair wasn't suited for
them and they wouldn't 'flatter' my
face. So I found a different stylist.

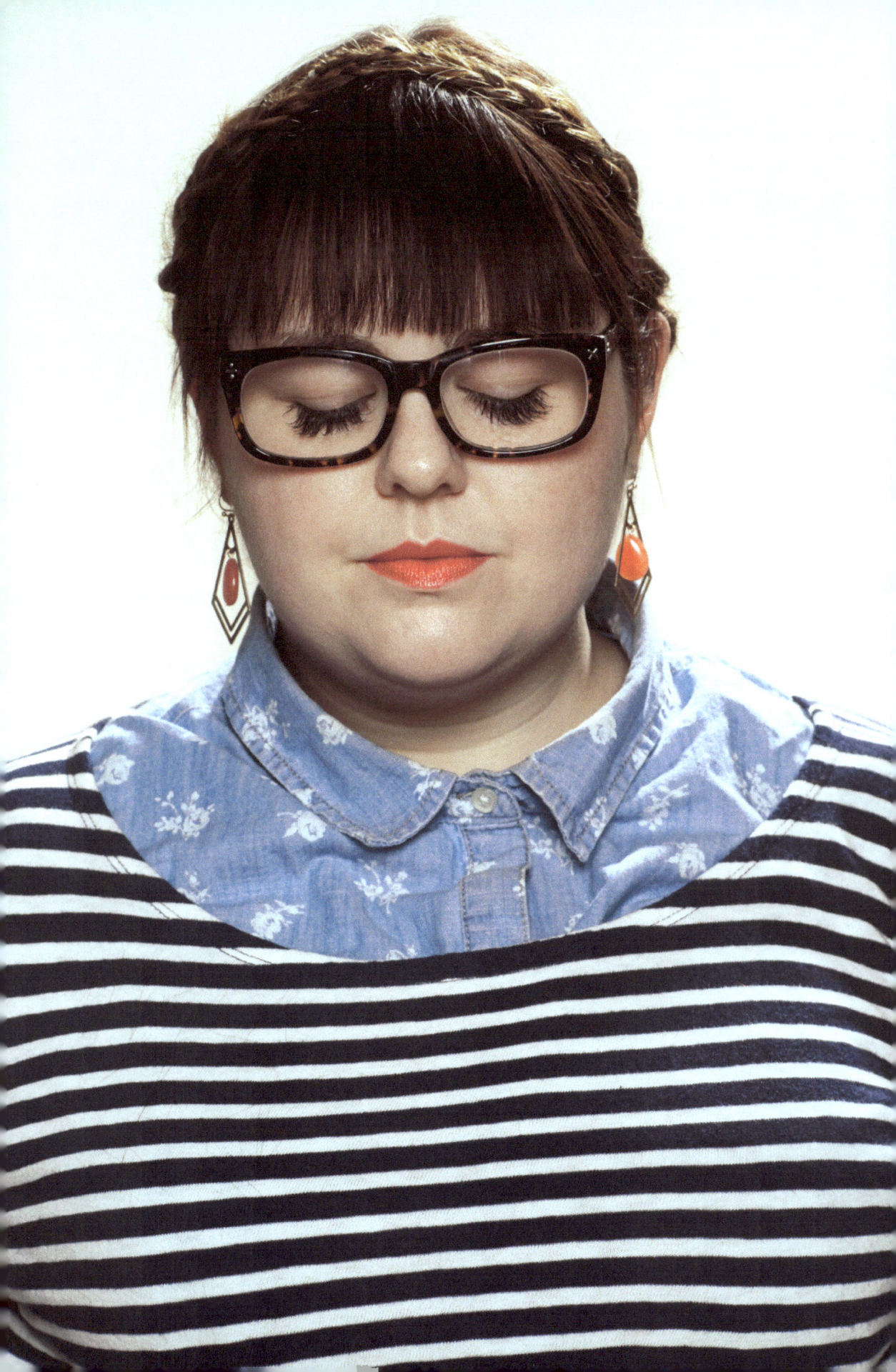

Photography
Sam Robinson

Creative
Rachael Jones

Retouching
The Laundry Room

Design
SEA

Hair
Heather Olexa
Sharon Hughes

Intro
Joanna Wilkinson

Acknowledgements
Amy Brooks-Schraub
Amy Ellis
Amy Kline
Arts + Labor
Christina & Byron Husch
Cj Vinson
Craig Lill
Dan Bailey
Dave Biediger
Freebirds World Burrito
Frock On Vintage
Jessica Nadeau
John Gorman
Kevin Russell
Ledbelly Vintage
Magsy
Matt Chauncey
Merita Zoga
Nora Hunter
Prototype Vintage Design
Ross Brind
Second Time Around
Shannon Gilmore
The Bus Stop Shop
The Niceties Of Life
Whitney Coulter

The Bangs
Valerie Aiello
Rhiannon Atkinson-Howatt
Kimberly Barrow
Amanda Barstow
Stephanie Bird
Stephanie Breijo
Audrey Brown
Baxter Buchanan
Sarah Elise Dominguez
Luisa Carneiro
Kitty Cash
Stephanie Castleberry
Kristen Catz
Natalie Collins
Whitney Coulter
Jackie Cueller
Megan Dombroski
Skyler Donias
Nikki Donlan
Mera Dougherty
Chris Drew
Frankie Estrada
Samantha Evans
Jacquelyn Feliz
Cristina Fisher
Trina Gear
Emily Glisson
Chelsea Gonzales
AJ Greenberg
Olivia Hjeritslev
Tiffany Hollon
Nicole Hute
Charly Janae
Brittany Keen
Lauren King
Knoxy Knox
Heather Labus
Lindsey Lee
Liz Lock
Tamara Lott
Alicia Lowery
Laurie Lyons
Esther Macas
Brittany Martin
Mandy May
Nairi Mila
Kirsten Mireles
Kelly Moore
Meghan Moore
Jessica Nadeau

Teresa Nichta
Jaimee Pierce
Erin Polsfoot
Tara Powell
Jocelyn Quintanilla
Zuleima Rodriguez
Alex Rose
Megan J Rutherford
Emily Saenz
Lori Salmon
Kelly Sampley
Courtney Severner
Kady Simmons
Marte S
Elizabeth Speights
Bryanna Stone
Lauren Tucker
Jennifer Vanek
Natalia Villarreal
Julie Wier
Casey Williams
Megan Young
Wenjing Zhang

www.ingramcontent.com/pod-product-compliance
Lightning Source LLC
Chambersburg PA
CBHW050852180526
45159CB00007B/2651